SCOOP

Tales and stories from four
decades as a sports journalist

NICK GARNHAM

First published 2015 by DB Publishing, an imprint of JMD Media Ltd,
Nottingham, United Kingdom.

ISBN 9781780914763

SCOOP

Tales and stories from four decades as a sports journalist

NICK GARNHAM

Foreword by
David Sheepshanks CBE

Acknowledgements

IN ALL the years I have known Bobby Flack he has only once ever given me an interview on the record.

So it is rather ironic that it was Bobby, the ex-Suffolk cricketer who is now coach to the county side, who encouraged me to write this book.

Bobby first suggested the idea four years ago, and each time he mentioned it the more I thought about it, before committing myself to the project.

However, none of this would have been possible without the backing of Steve Caron of JMD Media Ltd, who turned the idea into a reality.

The same applies to Terry Hunt, my former editor at the *East Anglian Daily Times*, who allowed me to dig deep into the archives to find old cuttings at the Ipswich offices of media group Archant.

My thanks also go to David Sheepshanks for writing the foreword. I thought long and hard who would be the right person to ask.

I wanted someone who shared my passion of football, and in particular Ipswich Town, but also cricket. And who better than David who, like myself, now works for The FA.

Thank also to my copy editor Paul Dalling and Jo Ward, who designed the front cover.

Finally, my thanks to my wife, Juliet, whose patience and proof-reading have also both been pivotal. My only concern now that *Scoop* has been published is that I no longer have any excuse for not doing all those jobs I have been avoiding around the house for the past 12 months.

The Author

THE third of four sons, Nick Garnham was born in Ipswich in 1961.

The sporting environment he grew up in plus his love of writing meant that once he realised he was never going to be good enough to be a professional footballer, after failing to even make the Ipswich West district side at the age of 11, Nick's heart was set on a career as a sports journalist.

After starting work with Eastern Counties Newspapers Ltd in July 1981, Nick spent five years as a news reporter with the *East Anglian Daily Times* and *Evening Star,* before landing a job on the sports desk in Ipswich shortly before his 25th birthday.

He spent the next 27 years covering local sport for the *East Anglian Daily Times, Evening* (later *Ipswich) Star* and *Green 'Un* Saturday football paper, specialising in covering cricket and non-league football.

Nick edited the *Green 'Un* for three years (1993–96) before becoming sports editor of the *East Anglian Daily Times* for nine years, and then head of sport for a further three years.

He then spent a further five years doing what he loved most – reporting on local sport – before the opportunity to take voluntary redundancy coincided with the offer of a job at Suffolk FA, where he has been marketing and public relations officer since May 2013.

He is married to Juliet and has two sons – Daniel and Ben – and one granddaughter, Gabrielle.

Foreword by David Sheepshanks CBE

NICK Garnham's long career at the *East Anglian Daily Times* and *Evening Star* virtually mirrored my own time span on the Board and then as Chairman of our beloved Ipswich Town Football Club.

What is perhaps less well known is that my love for cricket has also been lifelong and possibly even greater than that of football, although they do come close!

I can recall Nick as an eager young reporter when I was first given the honour of joining the Board at Portman Road in February 1987. The relationship between Directors and local press was, for the most part, a trusting and convivial one.

The sports reporters were allowed on the team coach to and from away matches, to stay in the same hotel, accompany pre-season tours and such like.

There was no shortage of stories, or laughs, such was the bonhomie and sense of fun around the Ipswich Board that I was so fortunate to join. And a conversation, 'off the record' was still possible in those days free of modern day demands and social media.

Nick has done brilliantly to capture the essence (and spirit!) of those times in these pages. No crisis at Portman Road unless the white wine had run out in the Boardroom!

It is extraordinary to think that we gave not one, but two managers to England, both to become legendary Soccer Knights of the Realm, qualified for Europe in nine of the ten years 1973–82 – would have been in the Champions League for most of them had it existed – and produced a string of International players between the mid-70s and 80s.

So, little wonder that Nick and I, each in our own ways, had tough acts to follow! But follow we did, never in my case with quite as much success as my Cobbold predecessors, as football progressively morphed from sport to business.

However, we maintained the traditions and the culture of the club and the stories kept on coming making this book a MUST read.

While Suffolk are a proud Minor Counties cricket team, most East Anglian cricket lovers have adopted Essex.

My own favourite player as a boy was Barry Knight, a fine all-rounder from Essex and England, though not quite in the Ian Botham mould. Trevor Bailey was the captain and a succession of great cricketers like Graham Gooch and Neil Foster have come off this production line to represent England since.

At Ipswich Town, we kept close links with Essex and I remember inviting Graham Gooch (notwithstanding him being an avid Hammer), when he was coach, to bring Essex pre-season training with our footballers in 2005–06. Andy Flower and a certain young Alastair Cook were present that day!

There's also a nice symmetry to our former Ipswich Town CEO, Derek Bowden, now being in charge at Essex County Cricket Club!

Reading *Scoop*, I thoroughly enjoyed this nostalgic stroll down memory lane and I hope you all enjoy it as much.

Introduction

'EVERYBODY does have a book in them, but in most cases that's where it should stay.'

Sorry to disappoint Christopher Hitchens, who is quoted above, but I decided to share my collection of stories, interviews and anecdotes gathered over the past 35 years.

Ever since I read Bill Naughton's *The Goalkeeper's Revenge* in my formative years I have yearned to write my own book.

After a few false starts, not to mention the passing of four-and-a-half decades, the realisation of a dream can be found within the pages of *Scoop*.

After turning 40 – the age where 'life begins' – I drew up my bucket list of 50 things to do.

Down at number 50 – not that it was in any particular order – was to write a book. Perhaps I subconsciously listed it last as I thought it would take me longer to achieve than anything else.

It was two totally unconnected events in the space of a fortnight in the summer of 2014 that convinced me to take the plunge.

A visit to the war graves in Ypres in Belgium – 100 years on from the Great War that claimed tens of thousands of lives – was particularly moving.

The death of my mother, aged 83, so soon after, was a reminder closer to home of how precious life can be.

They both served to inspire me to pull together this collection of stories, interviews and anecdotes covering my four decades as a local sports journalist.

The title *Scoop* was the nickname, by which I am still known to this day, that was given to me in cricketing circles because of my job as a journalist, and was reinforced when I scooped up seven catches in an innings for Copdock against Harwich & Dovercourt in a 2nd XI match in 1980.

This is still believed to be a record for all league cricket in Suffolk, but that's another story…

CONTENTS

Part One
– Starting Out

1. The Big Interview

TO all intents and purposes it was potentially the biggest interview of my life – none other than national treasure Sir Bobby Robson.

The former England manager still lived in Ipswich, home to the unfashionable club who he had guided to the giddy heights of annual title challengers in the old English First Division and a formidable force in Europe.

Robson had led Ipswich to their first – and to this day still their only – FA Cup final and plotted the downfall of favourites Arsenal at Wembley in 1978.

Three years later Ipswich lifted the UEFA Cup, defeating AZ Alkmaar 5–4 on aggregate, before Robson answered the call of his country.

His England side were defeated in the World Cup quarters-finals by a Diego Maradona inspired Argentina, albeit with help from the 'Hand of God' in Mexico 1986, and four years later reached the semi-finals in Italy only to bow out to Germany on penalties.

There then followed successful spells abroad in Holland, where he twice managed PSV Eindhoven, either side of stints with Sporting and Porto in Portugal and Spanish giants Barcelona.

Now, in September 1999, he was on the verge of a fairy tale return to management in England with his hometown club Newcastle United.

The story had broken that morning that the north-east club he had watched from the terraces as a boy wanted him, at the age of 66, as their new manager.

Mel Henderson, who used to be the public relations officer at

Portman Road in the Robson era, had been working on the sports desk of the *Evening Star* for several years.

He was still a good friend of Robson's and had rung him that morning to confirm the story, which had then run on the back page of that day's *Star*.

At that time the sports desks of the *Evening Star* and sister paper the *East Anglian Daily Times* and were run separately, and *EADT* editor Terry Hunt came over to the sports desk and we agreed to send a sports reporter and photographer round to Robson's house to get a one-to-one interview.

There was just one snag – I didn't have any members of staff available, meaning it would be down to me, the sports editor, to go and interview the great man!

That heady cocktail of excitement and nerves started to kick in as I prepared to leave the office with Paul 'Nick' Nixon, head of photographic at the *EADT*.

I had only ever met Robson once previously, several years before when he was at the town's Whitton Sports Centre for the launch of a community project, but other than a handshake and 'hello' I had never spoken to him.

The only other times I had been in his presence was on a couple of occasions when, in the 1975–76 season, I was an Ipswich Town ball boy and he had been interviewed before kick-off by Anglia TV commentator Gerry Harrison in the boot room where we changed just inside the entrance to the players' tunnel.

Although I couldn't claim to know Robson, I did have previous experience in interviewing a former England manager – none other than the great Sir Alf Ramsey, who led England to their 1966 World Cup triumph.

I had first met Sir Alf as a starry-eyed youngster when living in Cotswold Avenue in Ipswich – less than half-a-mile from his home on Valley Road.

Sir Alf was friends with Donald Gould, who lived a few doors down from us on the opposite side of the road, and one night I was invited round along with my brother Richard to meet him.

Then, a few years later when I was studying journalism at Harlow Technical College, I was able to ask Donald if he could arrange for me to have a one-to-one interview with Sir Alf.

I had requested if I could interview Sir Alf as part of my thesis on 'The Development of Ipswich Town Football Club' that I was writing as part of my coursework.

It just so happened that the year I was at college in 1980–81 coincided with the most memorable in the club's history, culminating in them winning the UEFA Cup, but narrowly failing to secure a remarkable treble as they finished runners-up to Aston Villa in the championship title race and lost to Manchester City in the semi-finals of the FA Cup.

My interview with Sir Alf was going to be the jewel in the crown of my thesis on how a small market town club in East Anglia, that only turned professional in 1936, had grown to be among the best in Europe.

While Sir Alf was happy to be interviewed, he told me that I could not, under any circumstances, directly quote him in my thesis as he was under contract to a national newspaper.

However, the interview with Robson promised to be something else.

'Nick' drove us round to Robson's house in Constitution Hill, like Ramsey's less than half-a-mile from where I used to live, and we agreed that I should approach the front door while 'Nick' waited behind me.

My heart was beating faster as my big moment arrived as the front door opened.

The face that appeared was not that of Robson, but his wife Elsie, who uttered the words that I have never been able to forget: "Are you the taxi driver?"

Perhaps I should have known that would happen; after all, I did have 'previous' when it came to interviewing another England manager – and that was before he was even bestowed the honour of leading his country.

It was while I was learning my trade at Harlow during that 1980–81 season that I saw an opportunity to interview one of my favourite footballers not only then, but even to this day.

Our journalism course required us to produce our own newspaper and fellow Ipswich Town fan Andy Totham, who came from Colchester, and myself took charge of the sports pages.

While Ipswich were drawn to play Manchester City in one semi-final of the FA Cup, Tottenham Hotspur were to meet Wolverhampton Wanderers in the other semi-final.

One of the stars of the Spurs side at the time was none other than Glenn Hoddle, who the previous season had been voted as the PFA Young Player of the Year.

And where was Hoddle born? You've guessed it, Harlow. I decided that would give us a back page scoop for our college newspaper – how Harlow's own son was aiming to reach Wembley.

So I set about organising an interview with Hoddle, which proved about as difficult as trying to play against the silky-skilled midfielder, who went on to win 53 caps for his country.

It took me no less than nine phone calls to the manager's secretary (Keith Burkinshaw was the Spurs boss at the time) before I had a date and time finally fixed for an interview.

This was to take place at Spurs' training ground at Cheshunt, which was about half-an-hour's train ride from Harlow.

I turned up in good time to see the last ten minutes of the training session before nervously approaching my subject as he came off the pitch and headed for the dressing rooms.

I introduced myself and said that I was there to interview him only for a bewildered-looking Hoddle to reply: "I know nothing about it."

He explained that he had a pre-arranged function to attend, but if I waited while he showered and changed he could give me ten minutes of his time.

That, if I am honest, was as much as I was expecting anyway – and it was ten minutes more than I got with Bobby Robson!

Despite Elsie's faux pas I still harboured hopes of an interview with the prospective new Newcastle United manager.

However, these were swiftly dashed by the great man himself as he appeared from behind his wife.

He explained that he was going to St James' Park to hear what Newcastle United had to offer and until he had met with club officials he could not say any more than that.

But Robson, ever the gentleman, ensured we didn't go away empty-handed, agreeing to pose on his front doorstep for a photograph which made the front page of the following day's *EADT*, before we passed the taxi driver – who else? – as we made our way back down the driveway.

So potentially the biggest interview of my entire career as a journalist never came to fruition, but on the plus side I can claim to have interviewed one past and one future England manager whilst still a teenager at college.

2. The apprentice

FIVE weeks – that's all it took – and one of those was spent on a pre-booked family holiday!

Just five weeks before I metaphorically put my foot right in it.

Let me explain. From the age of ten all I wanted to do when I left school was to be a sports reporter.

I have always regarded myself very fortunate to fulfil my dream, but before I did so I had to first train as a journalist and then serve my apprenticeship as a news reporter.

During my final year at Northgate Grammar School in Ipswich I applied for the position of a trainee journalist with Eastern Counties Newspapers, who had offices in both Ipswich and Norwich.

The office in Ipswich printed the *East Anglian Daily Times*, the morning newspaper covering Suffolk and north-east Essex, the *Evening Star,* the evening newspaper covering Ipswich and the neighbouring towns, the *Green 'Un*, the local Saturday night football newspaper, plus *The Mercury* series of weekly newspapers.

After undertaking an aptitude test and then an interview, I was one of four from around 80 applicants to be taken on by Eastern Counties Newspapers as a trainee journalist.

Along with my peers – Richard Cornwell, Dale Haste and Jeremy Lamb – I was among the intake of trainee journalists at Harlow Technical College in September 1980.

It was while at Harlow that along with Geoff Sutton, who later went on to work for *The Sun*, I lodged with a lovely landlady called Rachel Horton, who was in her 70s.

Thirteen years before, one of her previous lodgers was a young lad from the north-east of England who would sit up in his bedroom – the same one that I would later use – and play his guitar.

He went on to work for the *Yorkshire Evening Post* before becoming an international rock star. His name? Mark Knopfler, who co-founded, was lead guitarist, vocalist and songwriter of Dire Straits.

Coincidentally Dire Straits played at The Gaumont in Ipswich in December just after we had broken up for the Christmas holiday period.

When I told Rachel she wrote a letter which I passed on to a member of the road crew on the afternoon of the concert.

Six months later Rachel, who I wrote to regularly, received a phone call out of the blue from her former lodger, who apologised for not contacting her sooner as he had been touring.

After learning how to touch-type, shorthand, law, practical journalism plus local and central Government and successfully passing our end-of-year exams, we left college and started as trainee journalists.

I was posted to Felixstowe – and just five weeks into my job as a trainee journalist I put my foot in it big time.

News came through via the police that a lorry driver had crashed his vehicle, crushing his foot, at the Port of Felixstowe and I was assigned to the story.

The Port of Felixstowe, which is now the UK's busiest container port, is a massive complex, and with so little information to go on trying to find the lorry driver was like looking for a needle in a haystack.

However, we did have a home address – the street name but no house number – and so I was sent on my first door-knock.

It was late afternoon and not many people were at home, and those that were did not know where the injured driver lived.

By the following morning we had the name of the firm that the driver worked for, so photographer John Kerr and myself set off for the port.

We found the small family-run firm – the father and his injured son were the two drivers while the wife and mother ran the office – and I got some background and quotes.

By the time we got back to the office time was getting tight to first-edition deadline for that day's *Evening Star* and my chief reporter, Victoria Ainsworth, told me to read out what I had written in my notebook while she typed it out.

She topped-and-tailed the story and I then rang it through to the copytaker at head office in Ipswich with a few minutes to spare.

Job done. Or so I thought. A few minutes later Paul Durrant, who was running the news desk that morning, rang me back and said in his rich Brummie accent: "Is this some kind of sick joke?"

I was quite taken aback and wondered what on earth he was on about.

Durrant continued: "You've got a driver who has been so badly injured that his foot is hanging by a thread and he is facing the possibility of having it amputated and you've quoted the mother as saying he wanted to follow in his father's footsteps!"

Gulp. One major bollocking later, the offending quote was not surprisingly removed from the story before it was used in the second edition of that day's paper.

That gaffe may not have made it into print, but one I made a few months later actually did much to my embarrassment – and no doubt the person concerned, who just happened to be a local headmaster!

His name was Michael Matthews and he had just been appointed as the new head at one of Felixstowe's two high schools.

I went along to interview him and among the usual questions asked him if he had any hobbies or interests outside of work, before returning to the office, writing the story up and sending it off.

As well as filing stories for the *EADT* and *Evening Star*, each week we were responsible for producing copy to fill the *Felixstowe Times*, one of the aforementioned *Mercury* series of weeklies produced by the company.

Now while my intro – the opening paragraph of the story that is key to capturing the reader's attention – was altered for both the *EADT* and the *Star*, the original copy about Michael Matthews rearing chickens was not.

So on the front page of that week's *Felixstowe Times* appeared my original words: 'Among the hobbies of Deben High School's new headmaster is…raising his own meat.'

Ouch. It was only when the paper came out on the Friday morning and it was pointed out to me that I realised the double entendre.

It was one of those moments when I wished the ground would open up beneath me; I imagine Michael Matthews felt much the same.

Neither of my gaffes were considered so bad as to warrant disciplinary action, but let's just say my track record meant I was not considered one of the more promising trainee journalists the company had employed!

What my apprenticeship did do was to give me a good grounding in journalism, working as a trainee in not only the Felixstowe office but the larger West Suffolk office of Bury St Edmunds, before finally moving across to head office in Ipswich.

Being a news reporter, so far as I was concerned, was always a means to an end.

I made no secret of the fact that I craved the chance to switch to the sports department, and in April 1986 I seized my opportunity when I was offered a job in sport and started living the dream…

3. Rising stars

THE teenager on the other end of the telephone told me his biggest claim to fame was scoring a century for the MCC aged just 14 and five months. He politely explained that the MCC had turned up at his school one player short in May the previous year and he had been summoned from the classroom.

'My master in charge of cricket grabbed me out of the classroom and I batted at No.3 and scored 103 not out. After that I was selected to play for the 1st XI in every game!' he said.

Even though I was sports editor of the *EADT* at the time of the call in July 2000, I still made time to continue to write about cricket whenever possible.

So when a PR company rang in July 2000 to offer an interview with a member of the England squad who was from Essex and would be taking part in the Costcutter Under-15 World Cricket Challenge, I had readily agreed.

Hosts England were one of eight nations competing in the 50-overs-a-side competition starting at the end of the month.

The well-spoken youngster told me: "I was very pleased to be selected after all the hard work I put in. I hope to open the batting for England.

"It would be nice to play at Chelmsford in the semi-final because I haven't played there before – in fact, I haven't played on any county ground."

He concluded by saying that it would be a dream for everyone to reach the Final, which was being played at Lord's.

I often wondered what became of a host of rising stars that I interviewed who never hit the heights.

But that can't be said of the England Under-15 batsman from Wickham Bishops near Maldon.

His name, in case you haven't guessed already, was Alastair Cook, who is certainly the most high-profile sports person I have interviewed before they became famous.

Not only has he gone on to open the batting for England but also become captain and scored more Test centuries for his country than any other player. In May 2015 he passed his mentor Graham Gooch's tally of 8,900 runs to become England's leading Test run-scorer.

Cook's ability to grind down international attacks for hours on end is one of his greatest virtues and requires a great deal of patience, but it was a different kind of patience that Essex rising star Ben Foakes spoke of when I interviewed him at the club's Press Day in April 2011.

Foakes, the England Under-19 wicketkeeper and batsman, was all too aware that standing in his way at county level was James Foster, who was not only Essex captain but widely regarded as the outstanding wicketkeeper in the country.

The 18-year-old said: "Obviously I want to keep, but with someone like James Foster it is tough for me at the moment, so I will have to wait for and earn my chance."

Following his call-up for the England Lions tour to Australia in early 2013, I interviewed Foakes for a second time.

By then half-way through a two-year contract, Foakes said: "With James Foster being captain I am not going to be able to play as a 'keeper, but as long as I bat well and get chances and I work on my 'keeping with (coach) Barry Hyam and carry on improving and I am getting experience as a batsman, I don't see a problem.

"I would like to get into the side as a batsman and do as well as I can and then when Fozzie retires I will get my chance."

Sadly for Foakes, whose late father Peter Foakes was a former Football League referee, Foster's ability behind the stumps showed no signs of diminishing and nor did he show any desire to cut back on his workload.

With Foakes' options to keep wicket remaining limited, his patience had run out and it came as no real surprise when it was announced in August 2014 that he was leaving Essex to join Surrey.

While Foakes and team-mate Reece Topley were both England internationals from an early age, Tymal Mills only started playing cricket at the age of 14 – just five years before he made his first-class debut for Essex.

His rise from village cricket to that of first-class status was as rapid as the pace at which he was already bowling – and he clearly wanted to go higher.

"I am still only 18, so sometimes I have to pull myself back a little bit and just concentrate on improving. But I want to play for England one day," he told me.

Mills, who was born in Yorkshire but moved to Suffolk when he was only two-years-old, possesses a pair of the largest hands I have ever come across.

Indeed, when I interviewed him a year later at Essex's Press Day my Dictaphone he was holding slipped through his hand and smashed open on the concrete below, although fortunately it did not shatter.

By this time he had appeared for the England Lions in the fifth and final unofficial One-Day International against Bangladesh A.

But two frustrating summers followed at Essex before he, too, left the county at the end of the 2014 season, signing instead for Sussex.

Mills was certainly one of the most confident 18-year-olds I have come across, but I must confess I was taken aback when the phone rang on the *EADT* sports desk in November 1993.

The youngster on the other end of the phone was ringing to inform us that he had just signed a contract with Essex County Cricket Club.

In those days – long before the internet and social media – such a signing would normally be announced via a club Press Release sent in the post.

But this proud teenager decided to take the matter into his own hands. His name? Ashley Cowan, who was just finishing his education at Framlingham College.

The 18-year-old was keen to pay tribute to his mentor, Framlingham College cricket coach Colin Rutterford.

Cowan, who was laid low by a stress fracture of the back for seven months in 1992 and who was prevented from bowling by a dislocated knee for ten weeks the following summer, said: "Colin was the one who encouraged me at every opportunity.

"Colin drove me on, especially after my two injuries, as in my own mind I was prepared to give up – I thought I was not made for it."

Cowan, who was persuaded to go for a trial by ex-Essex spinner Ray East, who at the time was the Suffolk team manager, continued: "It is the chance of a lifetime. I have supported Essex for many years and I leapt at the chance of signing for the county."

Cowan went on to enjoy a successful career at Essex spanning 106 first-class and 148 List A matches, before major knee surgery effectively ended his career.

Josh Davey became the first home-grown Suffolk cricketer for a decade – the previous one was Justin Bishop – to earn a first-class contract when he signed a three-year summer deal with Middlesex in 2009.

The 19-year-old all-rounder told me: "My aim will be to win a full contract and break into the first team and one day to play for England."

Davey, who attended Culford School and played club cricket for Bury St Edmunds, did indeed go on to play international cricket – and with devastating effect.

He re-wrote the record books the following summer when he returned figures of 7.2-3-9-5 against Afghanistan – the best ever figures for a Scottish bowler in a one-day international – on only his fourth appearance.

However, Aberdeen-born Davey, whose family moved to Suffolk when he was aged just two, has so far failed to make much of an impact in first-class cricket.

He featured in just seven first-class matches for Middlesex before being released at the end of the 2013 season and then trying his luck with Somerset.

He impressed sufficiently to earn a contract at Taunton, and was selected for the Scotland side for the 2015 World Cup in Australasia, where at one stage he was the tournament's leading wicket-taker.

Matt Hunn was just 17 when he made his debut for Suffolk in the Minor Counties Championship and claimed three wickets against Buckinghamshire at Ipswich School in July 2011.

The following summer the 6ft, 5in fast bowler had his sights firmly set on a first-class career and told me: "I would like to think I am good enough.

"My coaches have said I do have a chance – I just have to work hard and put the hours in and hopefully I will get an opportunity."

That came just over a year later when he was left pinching himself after taking three wickets, including twice dismissing former South African batsman Ashwell Prince, on his first-class debut.

Hunn was hastily dual registered by Kent and handed his debut in their final LV County Championship Division Two fixture of the season against Lancashire at Canterbury.

He made national headlines when he picked up his maiden five-wicket haul in only his fourth first-class appearance in the opening match of Australia's 2015 tour of England.

4. Over and almost out!

"IF he kills you then at least I can say at your funeral that you died doing something you love," were my wife's comforting words as I set off from my home.

It was late September in 2011 and I was setting out on a sporting assignment with a difference.

Mark Heath, who had only been head of sport at Archant's Ipswich office for a couple of months, was clearly intent on making his mark, if you excuse the pun.

He had come up with the idea that I face an over from rising star Reece Topley, the Essex and England Under-19 bowler and then write a feature about it.

There were only two problems – Topley was 17 and I was 50 – plus aside from appearing in a couple of charity matches, I had not picked up a bat since retiring while Reece would have still been running around in his nappies!

So, after signing a risk assessment form and then raiding my loft to locate what little kit that remained, it was with some trepidation that I set off for the Topley home near Hadleigh in the Suffolk countryside.

Interviewing Reece was something I had become accustomed to, but facing him bowling was another matter altogether.

Reece and his dad Don, who I had known for many years, had invited me to the family home, where a net is erected in the back garden.

Don was concerned I had no chest or arm guard, and rummaged around inside Reece's kit bag for me to use equipment along with his helmet to make my appearance look more 'authentic' as he put it for the video camera that was to record the action. *

After a couple of 'sighters' Reece delivered the six balls, albeit off a shortened run as (fortunately for me) the garden was not long enough for him to bowl off his full run up.

I survived the over, even the bouncer Reece bowled with his fifth delivery, which I just ducked under as it flew over my left shoulder, even though I took my eyes of the ball.

It was a case of over and almost out, but it was ironic that I should end up batting in the nets against Reece just two years after I had first interviewed him following a net session that propelled him onto the front page of the *EADT*.

Reece was hit on the head by a Kevin Pietersen drive while bowling at England's batsmen as they prepared for the ICC World Twenty20 in this country in June 2009.

His father Don, himself a former Essex cricketer, had accompanied Reece to Loughborough University, where he had been invited to bowl in the nets.

Reece, a student at the Royal Hospital School at Holbrook, just outside Ipswich, was requested to attend to give England's batsmen practice against left-arm swing bowling, since they were expected to face several bowlers of this type in the tournament.

Topley Snr had tipped me off about his involvement that morning and I had arranged to speak to both him and Reece later in the day to give me an exclusive interview on his exploits.

But Don rang me back later that morning to tell me he was on his way to hospital with Reece, after Pietersen advanced down the wicket and unleashed a straight drive that had struck Reece on his left ear.

Although shaken up and groggy, Reece told me: "Despite suffering the injury I thoroughly enjoyed the experience. It was very challenging as they hit the ball so hard.

"Eoin Morgan was the hardest to bowl at because he wanders around the crease and also the different shots he plays.

"I found bowling at Kevin Pietersen there is a very small margin of error. You have to be careful not to give him too much width, or bowl too straight, because he also wanders across his crease.

"You have to be aware of how he moves and try to counter it when you bowl at him."

It was one of those stories that had snowballed and I rang the Press Association photographic desk, who I had spoken to earlier that morning to request pictures of Reece, to see what they had got.

They had some shots of Reece bowling, although none of the incident itself, but said they would make them available later in the day.

Reece, who had been due to sit two Year 10 internal exams at RHS that evening which the school had agreed he could miss earlier in the day, was instead left nursing a sore head after having several stitches inserted.

The *Daily Telegraph* also ran the story the next day, although without any quotes from Reece, and I subsequently wrote a follow-up picture-story when Pietersen autographed and donated his bat as he promised he would.

I subsequently interviewed Reece half-a-dozen times as I followed his fledgling career from the England age group sides through to his selection for the England Lions tour to Australia in early 2013.

After taking a five-wicket haul on his LV= County Championship debut against Kent, Reece repeated the feat against Middlesex in his next match in April 2011.

He faced a race against time to make the start of the return match at Chelmsford the following month, arriving just 20 minutes before the scheduled start after sitting an AS examination. He had to get special permission to sit a two-hour Business Studies exam at RHS, awaking at 6.30am and starting the exam just 75 minutes later, before being collected by dad Don and whisked the 36 miles to the County Ground.

Reece recalled: "I finished my exam at around 9.45 and it was then full on to Chelmsford. On the way I heard we were fielding so as soon as I arrived, I changed into my whites, went through a brief warm-up on the outfield and, minutes later, we were into the match."

In his rush to get to the game on time, Reece arrived minus his sweater, pointing the finger of responsibility at his father who had to go scurrying to the club shop to get a replacement.

"Because I came straight from school, my dad packed my bag and so it's his fault," he laughed.

He was less amused with his own initial efforts with the ball, sending down 16 overs for 80 runs without taking a wicket.

What was rather more amusing was how he came to hear of his call-up for the England Lions Tour to Australia in December 2012.

Rarely can a professional sportsman have gone from feeling so dishevelled to being so delighted as Reece did.

He was still recovering on the Sunday morning before Christmas from the effects of a party of a different kind, sleeping at a friend's house in Colchester with his phone switched off.

"I didn't get a phone call before the squad was announced, so I was totally unaware of what was happening," he revealed to me later.

A family friend called the Topley home on the Sunday morning to say that they must be chuffed about Reece's call-up, but Don and wife Julia were none the wiser.

Unable to contact him by phone for confirmation of the news, Julia picked up the Christmas turkey from Waitrose in Colchester, before going round to where Reece was staying and knocking on the door.

Reece answered the door to be told the news and subsequently said: "It was the last thing I was expecting. I was still recovering from the night before and when my mum called round and woke me up I was in shock and didn't believe her at first.

"It was totally out of the blue – I didn't even know the squad was being announced that morning."

*The video can be viewed via the following link: <u>http://www.eadt.co.uk/sport/cricket/video_our_man_faces_reece_topley_1_1082593</u>

Part Two
– Stars in their eyes

5. Location, location, location

EVEN now it seems slightly surreal.

One of England's best-loved cricketers lay there in his sick bed while answering my questions.

Derek Randall was the player in question, and the brief interview took place in an hotel in Kendal where Suffolk were staying while playing their opening Minor Counties Championship match of the 1994 season.

Randall had retired following an illustrious career the previous season and had signed to play for Suffolk in 1994, although he ended up being the county's professional for seven seasons.

His eagerly-awaited debut came in that season's two-day Championship opener against Cumberland at the picturesque venue of Kendal, although it turned into a match to forget for both Randall and Suffolk.

Randall, opening the batting with fellow debutant Glucka Wijersuriya, was dismissed for 13 in the visitors' first innings of 225 for eight declared, before Cumberland replied with 228 for five declared.

The match was then effectively won and lost inside the 13 overs of Suffolk's second innings before the close of play on day one, Mike Scothern doing the damage with a spell of five for 14 in 36 balls.

Ironically, Randall was the only Suffolk batsman who did not fall to Scothern – Marcus Sharp having him caught for 15, after also claiming his wicket first time around.

After being dismissed twice in a day, Randall set off out with his new team-mates for a curry that night.

The following morning I noticed he was not at breakfast and was told that he was not feeling well and was still in bed.

Back then I was required to file a fresh story for that day's *Evening Star* before the scheduled 11am start of play on the second morning of the match.

A combination of sensing a possible story and the fact that I was not sure whether I was the victim of a wind-up, I found out Randall's room number and went and knocked on the door.

His room-mate Wijersuriya, the Sri Lankan all-rounder, who after he had finished playing for Suffolk bought Shenley Cricket Ground in Hertfordshire, answered in his customary polite manner.

There, indeed, was Randall lying flat in bed with the covers pulled right up to his neck.

I stood in the doorway and carried out a brief interview to verify the fact that Randall was under the weather as a result of something he had eaten in the Indian restaurant the night before.

It was just as well that Randall had been dismissed the previous evening as he was in no fit state to bat on that second morning, stopping the runs rather than scoring them was his immediate priority!

In the event, Sharp swept aside the Suffolk tail and Cumberland knocked off the 70 runs required either side of lunch to wrap up a comfortable nine-wicket win.

While interviewing Randall on his sick bed ranks as the most unusual setting for an interview, meeting a future international coach in a McDonald's restaurant was not far behind.

The McDonald's in Cowdray Avenue, close to Colchester and East Essex's Castle Park ground, is where I met up with former Essex bowler Ian Pont, who went on to be Bangladesh bowling coach.

At the time Pont was a partner in Hogger Sports, a market leader in coloured clothing who had supplied replica kits for the 1992 World Cup in Australasia.

Hogger Sports had won the contract to supply the kit to all 18

English counties for the AXA Equity Law League in England in the summer of 1993, the first time coloured clothing was to be worn in the UK.

I had arranged to meet Pont to do an article on the revolutionary move, and he suggested meeting at McDonald's, as finding my way to the adjacent Castle Park was the only place I really knew in the town.

Pont tucked into an egg McMuffin as we chatted, before taking me outside and opening his car boot to reveal the various different designs that the counties would be wearing that summer!

Former Essex batsman Nick Knight subsequently wore the blue coloured clothing of England during his 100 one-day international appearances.

In April 2004 Knight, who was then the captain of Warwickshire, was making a flying visit to Felsted School in Essex, where he was educated, and had agreed an interview.

The meeting had been arranged through Mark Surridge, a house master at Felsted School and himself a useful club cricketer.

Surridge's study room was the unusual location where I met with Knight on a Sunday afternoon prior to his first season as skipper.

During our interview Knight, who had retired from international cricket the previous year, said: "It is a good time to be captain – whilst I say it now I probably won't be saying it in August – but we have got several young players with a lot of ability."

Knight's fears were unfounded as he led them to the county championship that summer.

The dining room of another public school was the equally unusual venue for my interview with Geoff Miller, who at the time was National Selector of the England cricket team.

Miller was the guest speaker at a luncheon at Ipswich School, where Suffolk were staging a fund-raising event during a Minor Counties match.

The school dining room was in stark contrast to the plush

surroundings of Hintlesham Hall Hotel, the Grade I Listed Elizabethan Manor House located just outside Ipswich.

It was there that I interviewed Nasser Hussain, who at the time was captain of England, and had agreed to be guest speaker at a charity lunch in April 2002.

The function had been organised by Caroline Byatt, who used to handle the PR at Essex County Cricket Club during Peter Edwards' time as secretary/general manager, but was now working for the Suffolk Preservation Society.

She had coaxed Hussain into being the guest of honour and had contacted me to ask if I would conduct a Q&A session.

In return I had asked if Hussain would be interviewed beforehand, and my reward was a lengthy interview and enough copy to fill two pages.

6. Ladies and gentlemen

STRIPPER Bianca, clad in only a G-string, was halfway through her routine when a member of the audience got up from his chair and on to the stage.

Another member of the cheering crowd of around 250 boozed-up punters reacted by getting up and bundled him off the stage.

This was the catalyst for Bianca to flee the stage as fighting broke out and bottles were thrown across the room.

The police were called and the saucy strip show at one of Suffolk's top hotels came to a shuddering halt.

The irony was that the 'Gentlemen's Evening' had been organised by the football club at Willis Faber, now known just as Willis, a global company and the world's oldest insurance broker.

I was on a table with work colleagues and still learning my trade in the newsroom at the time, and the following day was tasked with writing a front-page story on the ugly drunken brawl.

Hotel general manager Simon Jackson told me it was the first time that the police had been called to a private function at the four-star Ipswich Moat House at Copdock, just outside Ipswich.

Well-known Ipswich-based comedian Micky Zany pulled no punches when he said: "I could feel the tension half-way through the evening, and it didn't surprise me in the least when there was a scuffle.

"It was one of the worst stag nights I have ever done, and I have done a few."

Over the years I have attended countless functions at the venue, now known as the Cameo Hotel, but none quite like the one described above.

That was the only 'Gentlemen's Evening' as such, with the vast majority Sporting Dinners with guest speakers and a whole host of comedians.

From the world of cricket I have listened to Jonathan Agnew, Peter Baxter, Dickie Bird, Henry Blofeld, Sir Ian Botham, Geoffrey Boycott, Chris Broad, Chris Cowdrey, Ray East, Graham Gooch, Sir Richard Hadlee, Nasser Hussain, Ronnie Irani, Allan Lamb, Dennis Lillee, Christopher Martin Jenkins, Vic Marks, Geoff Miller, Chris Old, Derek Randall, Dermot Reeve, Sir Viv Richards, Sir Garfield Sobers, David Steele, Don Topley and Fred Trueman.

From the world of football I have heard speak Alan Ball, Gordon Banks, Peter Beardsley, George Best, Stan Bowles, Alan Brazil, Sir Trevor Brooking, Steve Bull, Jack Charlton, Martin Chivers, Steve Claridge, George Cohen, Pat Crerand, Martin Dobson, Tommy Docherty, David Fairclough, Ricky George, Jimmy Greaves, Ron Harris, Matt Holland, John Hollins, Roger Hunt, Sir Geoff Hurst, Norman Hunter, Pat Jennings, Craig Johnston, Graham Kelly, Howard Kendall, Steve Kindon, Denis Law, Matt Le Tissier, Gary Mabbutt, Lou Macari, Malcolm Macdonald, Rodney Marsh, Duncan McKenzie, Lawrie McMenemy, Jan Molby, Frank McLintock, John Motson, Alan Mullery, Peter Osgood, Gavin Peacock, Steve Perryman, Martin Peters, David Platt, Mick Quinn, Harry Redknapp, Graham Roberts, Ian St John, David Sheepshanks, Peter Shilton, Nobby Stiles, Mike Summerbee, Gordon Taylor, Norman Whiteside, Bob Wilson and Frank Worthington.

From the world of rugby I have listened to legends Bill Beaumont, Gareth Edwards and Willie John McBride and also to athletics coach Frank Dick.

And they are just the ones I can remember!

They all have their own sporting tales to tell, and some have been better than others, but one sticks out in my memory above all else, although not as a speaker.

They say you should never meet your heroes, but when I heard Matt Le Tissier was coming to Ipswich I could not resist interviewing my football idol.

My admiration for 'Le Tiss' was based on the fact that he played the way I would have loved to have played the Beautiful Game – a true artist among artisans.

He only won eight England caps, a measly return for someone so gifted and who scored 162 goals, including some of the most spectacular in Premier League history, in 443 appearances as an attacking midfielder for Southampton between 1986 and 2002.

Le Tissier and QPR manager Harry Redknapp were the guest speakers at Felixstowe & Walton United's 25th Sportsman's Dinner, held at the aforementioned Cameo Hotel at Copdock, in April 2013.

I found out via the club that the person who had booked Le Tissier was none other than Barry Dye, a well-known entertainments agent in Ipswich who also happens to be my wife's godfather.

Barry spoke to Le Tissier who agreed to the interview before the dinner, except that he eventually arrived too late to do it before the assembled 300 guests sat down.

Le Tissier rather sheepishly admitted that the reason he was late was because he had been to his former Southampton team-mate Richard Hall's house for a cup of tea on the other side of Ipswich and forgotten he was doing the interview.

However, he promised to do have a chat when the starters were served and was true to his word so we sat down to talk in the foyer where it was much quieter.

Le Tissier had always given the impression of being a very laid-back character on the field, and he was no different off it.

How would he have fared in the Premier League today, bearing in mind the improved fitness of the players compared to in his heyday?

"I would always back myself to be able to influence a football match whether I could run fast or not. If you have got enough ability you can get away without having blistering pace to influence a game," he replied.

And did he wish he was playing now, considering the wages earned by Premier League players compared to when he played?

Le Tissier said: "There is a generation of players who were playing before we were who would not have minded a bit of that.

"With the amount of money they earn now comes a lot of other pressures, so I am quite happy to have played in the era that I did.

"The money players earn today would have been nice, but I have no complaints that I played in the era that I did and I am pretty happy with my life as it is now."

He certainly came across as the down-to-earth individual I always thought – and hoped – that he would be.

The interview only lasted around ten minutes, and was even interrupted by a couple of the evening's guests asking to be photographed with Le Tissier.

After-dinner speaking is an art and one that not everyone is cut out to do, so I was taken aback when I was approached to be the guest speaker at a charity golf event in September 2010.

The dinner followed on from a day's golf at Hintlesham Hall Golf Club in aid of Marie Curie Cancer.

Surely the organisers had got me mixed up with former sports editor Tony Garnett, who was the golf correspondent for the *EADT* and *Evening Star*?

No, it was me who they wanted to be the guest speaker, so I agreed after failing to find a good enough reason to talk them out of it.

In front of around 200 people I rather nervously delivered my speech, a snap-shot of my career as a sports journalist.

I included the story of my hair-raising experience when I was invited to sit alongside the driver and do a few laps around Foxhall at the Press Day for the forthcoming Spede Weekend that included the Hot Rod World Championships.

As I got in the car I recalled that the co-driver threw me a toilet roll and quipped: "You might need this" and he wasn't joking either!

And I finished with my favourite headline ever to appear in the *EADT* which was written by my former colleague Lee Dinmore, a young lad who worked as a sub-editor on the sports desk.

Lee never owned up as to whether it was intentional or not, but knowing Lee as I did I wouldn't mind betting he knew exactly what he was doing.

The point-to-point copy Lee was subbing mentioned there were so many first-time runners that one of the races had to be divided, giving Lee licence to write: 'Maiden split in two by huge entry'.

7. Sporting legends

IAN BOTHAM is widely regarded as England's greatest ever all-rounder.

A total of 14 centuries and 383 wickets – a record that stood after he played the last of his 102 Tests in August 1992 until it was broken by James Anderson as recently as April 2015 – are testament to his outstanding talent.

But when I interviewed him in late 1992, 'Beefy' claimed to have no thoughts of retiring from the international stage.

He was visiting Ipswich with his old pal, former West Indies skipper Viv Richards, as part of their *The King and I* nationwide stage tour.

Although he had made himself unavailable to tour India and Sri Lanka that winter, Botham said he was still keen to play Test cricket.

"The Australians are here next summer and I am looking forward to that. I am nowhere near finished. I am only 36 and have a lot of cricket left in me.

"We seem to have a problem in this country of writing everyone off once they get past 30," he told me.

Would a home Test Series against South Africa, provisionally earmarked for 1994 following their return to the international arena, provide a fitting finale to his career, I wondered?

"I'll decide that," came Bonham's terse reply down the phone, leaving me in no doubt it was time to change the subject.

It was a full 16 years later that I interviewed Richards, who by then was a Sir, like Botham, when he spoke at a Sporting Dinner.

Richards and ex-Essex skipper Ronnie Irani were the guest speakers at the event at what is now the Cameo Hotel at Copdock just outside Ipswich.

I was granted a ten-minute slot to speak to the pair and Irani, who I had spoken to several times before, sensed that this was a once in a lifetime chance for me to interview Sir Viv.

So I was extremely grateful to Ronnie when he told me to address my questions to the cricketing knight as I could interview Irani at any time, and I didn't need a second invitation.

Did Sir Viv think Test matches were under threat from Twenty20 cricket?

"Test match cricket was always the best way to test whatever skills you have as a cricketer – it was always the ultimate test," he replied.

"What I do know is that if cricket needs to stay alive as a mainstream sport and entertainment, it is important that we continue to play and appreciate Test match cricket.

"However, if cricket is to prosper we need to put more bums on seats and if we can do this through Twenty20 it will help it to survive and then we can still play the traditional game as well as the Twenty20 format."

In April 1997 I found myself in the company of another cricketing Knight, this time Sir Richard Hadlee, who was speaking at Bury St Edmunds Cricket Club's Gentlemen's Evening.

Hadlee cut a very relaxed figure when we spoke at his hotel ahead of that evening's engagement in the West Suffolk town.

Plans were afoot to extend the county championship from three-day to four-day fixtures (from 1988 to 1992 some matches were four days before all matches became four days in 1993) and it was a move he backed.

Hadlee played in the county championship for Nottinghamshire from 1978–87, but he only figured in three full seasons due to injuries and Test calls.

Notts won the title in two of those summers – 1981 and again in 1987.

He said: "A two-division county championship would make the standard that much higher – promotion and relegation would give everyone a greater incentive to keep performing.

"Change is all part of living as you have to keep pace and be prepared to make changes or you will get left behind by all the others who are making changes."

Wise words indeed, much the same as former Australian fast bowler Dennis Lillee, who I interviewed ahead of his visit to the Corn Exchange in Ipswich for an evening of cricketing memories with Derek Randall and Geoff Miller in October 1993.

England were touring the West Indies that winter and Lillee said they had their best chance of a series success for 15 years, although they would miss the 'Gooch Factor' as Graham Gooch was not touring the Caribbean.

Lillee told me: "You cannot replace a batsman like Gooch overnight. He is basically an institution in English cricket and one of the finest opening batsmen in the world and you are going to miss a player like that.

"However, Alec Stewart is capable of doing a very good job at the top end of the order and if he strikes form he will take the West Indies on."

England got themselves in good positions in each of the first four Tests, but failed to capitalise as West Indies won the series 3–1, Stewart scoring twin centuries in England's 208-run victory in the Fourth Test in Barbados.

Gooch was indeed an institution for both Essex and England, and someone who I have interviewed half-a-dozen times over the years.

The first time was in 1993 after his Essex side had defeated Suffolk in their NatWest Trophy first-round tie in front of more than 4,000 spectators at the Victory Ground in Bury St Edmunds.

As a line of autograph hunters formed an orderly queue to obtain his signature, I decided the only way to speak to him was to join the end of the line.

The only problem was that when I approached Gooch with my notebook and pen in hand he thought I was after his autograph as well!

What I liked about him was that after scoring a record 67,057 runs – 44,846 first-class and 22,211 one-day runs – and captaining both his county and country, Gooch was still very down to earth.

After returning to Essex as first-team coach I interviewed him at Chelmsford in February 2002, and asked if it had taken much persuasion for him to return to his roots?

He replied: "Persuasion is not the right word. I had set out on a different path. I was coaching up until two years ago with England and had worked for Durham on a part-time basis since I finished playing.

"I had been doing a lot of media work, which was very enjoyable, and although my heart has always been in Essex I didn't expect to be invited back, but I was delighted to take up the challenge."

Fast forward eight years and Gooch was still clearly getting his kicks from cricket – and still humbled to be involved.

The then 56-year-old was batting coach to Essex and had been invited to assist England initially on a temporary basis for their four-Test series in South Africa, which was then extended.

He said: "It is great to still be involved working with the Essex players and going back to England is a great thrill for me."

Another Essex and England captain I interviewed was Nasser Hussain after he had returned from an arduous winter touring Zimbabwe, India and New Zealand in 2002.

Despite the honour of captaining his country Hussain admitted he missed his 'soul mates' and being an Essex boy.

He said: "I have to be honest and say I don't miss the day in, day out travelling aspect, but I do miss the closeness of that dressing room.

"They have always been my boys and I have always been one of their boys."

Hussain said there were different eras – at first it was himself, John Stephenson, Derek Pringle, Nadeem Shahid and Nick Knight who used to go round together. Then it became Mark Ilott, Ronnie Irani and Paul Grayson.

"England is slightly different. England is high pressured, because this is your job, you are doing it for your country.

"But you do miss the day in, day out banter with your real soul mates that you have grown up with.

"It is very difficult when you only pop in for a month of the season to regain the banter and know what's going on off the field and on the field, so I do miss that.

"That will hopefully come back as I'm not going to play for England forever."

Hussain played the last of his 96 Tests in May 2004 – just over two years later – scoring an undefeated 103 and hitting the winning runs against New Zealand at Lord's.

He announced his retirement from all cricket, instead joining the Sky Sports commentary team on a full-time basis, rather than return to the treadmill of the county circuit.

While Hussain called time on performing at the highest level, another England captain was showing no signs of slowing down when we spoke. Charlotte Edwards was visiting Suffolk in late 2008 to coach the next generation of cricketers.

Only two months before she had won the women's prize at the International Cricket Council Player of the Year awards.

She had by then been playing international cricket for 12 years, captained her country and won the Ashes twice.

Edwards said: "There is so much more I still want to do. I want to lead the country for a number of years, keep on winning and be the most successful captain I can be.

"People say I have done a lot in the game but I feel like I am playing the best cricket I have ever played so I just want to keep on breaking more and more records and be successful for England."

Edwards, who said she wanted to win a World Cup, did so the following year, captaining England to victory over New Zealand in the Final in Australia.

She then led England to the World Twenty20 title at Lord's in 2009, before retaining the Ashes against Australia.

Edwards has continued to break records and raise the bar so far as the women's game is concerned.

"I plan to play for as long as I can, because I have spoken to a lot of people and you are a long time retired and I think you get better as you get older, especially as a batter, so I just hope my body holds out for me!" she said.

It's certainly been a case of so far, so good, for England's record-breaking women's captain.

Mention of record-breaking England internationals leads me to Bobby Charlton, one of the greatest midfield players of all-time, who I interviewed while working on the news desk in April 1985.

Charlton, who was knighted in 1994, brought his sports and soccer school sponsored by TSB to Ipswich for a two-day course at Thurleston High School.

Around 100 youngsters attended the course, and Bobby told me: "There will be some good players emerge from here. I have seen about half-a-dozen who have a good chance of going on to clubs."

I don't know whether any did go on to join a club, but even if they did no-one would have matched the achievements of Charlton, who won 106 caps, scored a record 49 goals and was a member of England's 1966 World Cup-winning side – a sporting legend indeed.

8. *Opportunity knocks*

THE former Test cricketer sat opposite looked anything other than the tortured soul whose marital problems had been splashed across several tabloid newspapers.

Dressed in a grey suit and open-necked shirt, the ex-England batsman appeared very relaxed as he sat in one of the new changing rooms of Mildenhall Cricket Club's refurbished pavilion, which he had just officially opened, in May 2009.

He was happy to chat for as long as it took, and also to answer questions on all manner of topics.

Although one of my favourite cricketers, I was not sure how approachable Graham Thorpe would be, bearing in mind some of the treatment he had received from the media.

But when I heard he was visiting Suffolk it was too good a chance to pass up, even though I was officially on holiday and it was a two-hour round trip with no guarantee that I would get an interview.

I need not have worried. Thorpe's troubled past, which saw him exiled from the international arena, had been left firmly behind.

He spoke about how he felt Australia were favourites for the forthcoming Ashes Series, how he believed Test cricketers would retire earlier in the future to prolong their international careers in the shorter versions of the game and even spoke openly about the pressures associated with playing at the top level.

Marcus Trescothick had been forced to retire prematurely following a stress-related illness, Steve Harmison's homesickness while away on tours had been well-documented while Matthew Hoggard had revealed he thought he was 'going cuckoo' while touring after his wife suffered post-natal depression.

Thorpe said he felt an understanding and education was needed for players that when they got on the treadmill of international cricket they understood where it was going.

He explained: "I think we are not quite as harsh on it as we used to be ten or 15 years ago. There is more of an understanding that players' personalities are all different and they all need a support mechanism.

"I think that support mechanism is better, but ultimately it is still a sport at the highest level which in a way puts you under pressure and you need good people around you."

But Thorpe also said that cricketers should not lose sight of how fortunate they are to be performing at international level.

"You need to put it into perspective for what it is. Although I had pressures on the outside, sometimes I knew I was very lucky to be playing cricket, and if players can keep that in the forefront of their mind it helps.

"You are on the road a long time and you can forget you are doing something which people would die to do, which is the important thing."

The chance to interview someone such as Thorpe was the type often afforded to journalists, such as when a celebrity visits your patch to speak at a dinner, perform an opening ceremony or promote a product.

Opportunity knocked in such situations – and a few weeks later that was also the case when the all-star Lashings international side appeared at Culford School, near Bury St Edmunds.

Although a baking hot Sunday afternoon on my weekend off, I was not going to pass up the chance to interview former Australian Test star Jason Gillespie just before that summer's first Ashes Test.

Unlike Thorpe, who was left out of the 2005 series and replaced by Kevin Pietersen, Gillespie played in the Ashes Series as a member of the Australian side that lost one of the great series of all time.

It was the only time in five Ashes series that the former fast bowler, who later coached Yorkshire and was widely tipped to coach England before fellow Aussie Trevor Bayliss was appointed as Peter Moores successor in May 2015, ended on the losing side.

As we stood inside an empty marquee, I asked Gillespie, who became the first acknowledged Aboriginal person to play Test cricket, what it would be like inside the Australian dressing room before the opening match in Cardiff.

He said: "There will no doubt be some nerves. As with any series it is very exciting but for Australians it is something special playing against England in an Ashes Series.

"I think it is more the anticipation rather than nerves – you have nerves before every game, that is part and parcel of cricket – but the anticipation of what the series could be like and how it could unfold is an unknown.

"But you dream of playing for your country and that opportunity to be involved is phenomenal."

As the first acknowledged Aboriginal person to play Test cricket, did the Ashes mean more to him than other Australians?

"I am a very proud Aboriginal and a very proud Australian and any time you represent your country – and that is not disrespecting the Ashes in any way – it doesn't matter who you play against, but the fact that you are wearing your country's colours is a very proud moment.

"As an Aboriginal person it is something that you dream of from a very young age and I was fortunate to be able to play cricket for Australia," he replied.

Mike Gatting knows not only what it is like to play in an Ashes Series but also to skipper his side to victory Down Under.

The ex-Middlesex batsman visited Ipswich Cricket Club, which had been chosen as a 'showcase' club for the ECB's NatWest Cricketforce scheme at the start of that same summer, in early April 2009.

Asked what he thought the outcome of the forthcoming Ashes Series would be, Gatting was spot on when he replied: "I think there are going to be results and it will be something like 2-1 to England."

Gatting gave me enough copy to write a two-page feature, but I sensed he felt he had fulfilled his media obligations when I later asked him if I could shoot some video for our website.

He did agree to do the interview, so would have been less than amused to learn that it was never uploaded onto the website due to a staff shortage in the web team because of holidays!

That same day Sussex all-rounder Luke Wright was also at Ipswich CC, and was relishing the prospect of playing in that summer's ICC World Twenty20 tournament in England.

"It should be so exciting if it is anything like the last Twenty20 World Cup in South Africa. It will be a great event but I hope we can perform better than we did then," he enthused.

Wright top-scored with 71 for England in their opening match at Lord's against the Netherlands but was powerless to prevent a four-wicket defeat and their subsequent elimination at the group stage.

The 24-year-old had stepped in at short notice to travel to Ipswich, after England off-spinner Graeme Swann was forced to cancel his scheduled visit.

It was to be another two-and-a-half years before I finally spoke to Swann, who was offered up for a telephone interview to promote a charity auction and ball being organised in memory of former England football manager Sir Bobby Robson.

Swann is a lifelong fan of Newcastle United – the club where Robson, who hailed from the north-east, brought down the curtain on his illustrious career as a manager.

He met Robson shortly before he died in July 2009 following a long battle with cancer, and Swann was donating VIP hospitality for the following summer's Lord's Test against the West Indies as well as a signed England shirt from that match for the Sir Bobby Robson Foundation and cancer charity Suffolk Breakthrough.

But in addition to plugging the event, I was eager to ask Swann what he remembered about his Minor Counties debut.

He was just 17 and taking his first steps to stardom when he made his bow for Bedfordshire against Suffolk at Ransomes Sports Ground in Ipswich in June 1996, but could he recall the match?

To my surprise he replied: "I do – I am blessed with a good memory for cricket matches. It was against Suffolk at Ransomes and we clung on for a draw in the end.

"Suffolk had a good left-arm spinner and it was a turning wicket. I got 20 or 30 in our second innings."

The spinner Swann referred to was Andrew Golding, who claimed Swann's wicket in his haul of six for 75, after the No.9 had made 34 off 51 balls.

Swann did not bat or bowl on the opening day of the two-day fixture, but took three wickets in Suffolk's second innings, including that of ex-England batsman Derek Randall.

I have never enjoyed interviews over the telephone, especially if I was writing a feature-length article and particularly if it was someone whom I had never previously met.

So interviewing Mark Ramprakash in August 2012 while he was driving on the motorway with poor reception was one of my more challenging assignments.

Ramprakash was the star name among a team of former England cricketers who were heading to Ipswich Cricket Club to play as the PCA England Masters in a charity fundraising match.

Despite winning 52 Test caps and becoming one of only 25 players to score 100 first-class centuries, Rampraskash had become accustomed to more people wishing to talk to him about the 14 weeks he spent appearing on a TV show than his 25 years as a professional cricketer!

Ramprakash, of course, had wowed the prime-time television audience in 2006 when he won the *Strictly Come Dancing* title with partner Karen Hardy.

But Ramprakash, who had announced his retirement from first-class cricket the previous month, was philosophical about the public's perception of him.

"Cricket people will remember me for my cricket career first and foremost, but you have to accept that *Strictly* is a mainstream television programme.

"Around 12 million people watched the Final and you are in a totally different bubble. I had a great time and I will remember it fondly. I was very lucky to be paired with a lovely lady, but I took *Strictly* for what it is," he explained.

Part Three
– The boys of '78

9. Bacon and Eggs

CHELSEA had Ron 'Chopper' Harris, Leeds United had Norman 'Bite Yer Legs' Hunter and Liverpool had Tommy 'Iron Man' Smith. Ipswich Town had Allan Hunter.

'Big Al', as he was affectionately known, was one of football's hard men – a breed of player who struck fear into the opposition in the 1970s.

Hunter made more than 350 appearances for Ipswich between 1971 and 1982, and played a pivotal role in the club's 1978 FA Cup Final victory over Arsenal at Wembley in 1978.

Hunter's crunching tackle on Frank Stapleton inside the opening ten seconds set the tone for Town's triumph beneath the Twin Towers.

I had never met Hunter before, let alone interviewed him, when I arrived at his house, less than a mile from my own home, one dank January morning in 2008.

The purpose of my visit was the latest in a series of interviews with every member of that cup-winning team to mark the 30th anniversary of the club's only FA Cup success.

I went inside and offered to remove my shoes, but Hunter assured me there was no need.

I was shown into his lounge and sat down – only to realise the trail of dirty footprints I had left behind me on the carpet.

Hunter and wife, Carol, had recently replaced two of their radiators and I had unwittingly stepped in some of the sludge and sediment mixed in with the rain on the driveway outside and carried it indoors on the soles of my shoes!

It was an inauspicious start to the interview, but over the course of the next hour-and-a-half the centre back nicknamed 'The Strange Man' by his team-mates was convivial company.

He revealed that, even three decades later, he did not know why he had fisted the ball away in the 76th minute when Town were winning 2-0 in the semi-final at Highbury against West Bromwich Albion who scored from the resultant penalty.

Such was the aura that surrounded Hunter, several of his colleagues had since confessed they dared not ask him what he was doing!

Hunter said: "It was a good job they didn't ask me because I could not have told them why I did it.

"Maybe it was the Irish in me. They always say the Irish are a bit mad! I guess I just had a brainstorm – I could do that occasionally."

John Wark's goal in the dying seconds sealed Town's place at Wembley against Arsenal, with Hunter only being passed fit to play on the morning of the Final itself.

Hunter, who was 30-years-old at the time, recalled: "I remember Danny Blanchflower (who had been Hunter's Northern Ireland manager) coming to the hotel to do a television interview. He said to me 'If you were 23 I would tell you to forget about it, but this could be your last chance, so if you think you can play then do so.'"

Despite passing an 8.30am fitness test on the hotel lawn, Hunter admitted he was frightened he might get a reaction right up to kick-off.

"If the truth be known I was doubtful right up until five o'clock!" he quipped.

Hunter's parents, Mary and Albert, were there to see the Final – the only time his mum ever travelled out of Ireland – and Hunter made his presence felt before he even got on the pitch.

While the two teams were waiting in the tunnel to go out, Arsenal striker Malcolm Macdonald spoke to him and said, "May the best team win", but Hunter just glared back at him.

"It did the job and intimidated him," said Hunter, who instantly remembered that tackle on Stapleton when I brought it up in conversation.

"I wanted him to know I was around. It was in a lot of defenders' make-up to hit your opponent hard early on, and they would then always be looking for you after that. It was part of your game plan as was having chit-chat with certain players, telling them what you were going to do to them.

"It was all psychological. I was not tougher than anyone else. I suppose you could say it was bullying, although I don't like to use that term, but if you could intimidate someone then you did. Some players you could get through to, but others told you to **** off."

Hunter's central defensive partner was Kevin Beattie, and the pair were dubbed 'Bacon and Eggs' by manager Bobby Robson.

Beattie, like Hunter, still lives in Ipswich, so interviewing the man widely regarded as the club's greatest-ever player should have been relatively straightforward.

Not so. Beattie twice stood me up before we finally sat down together at his home in the town.

Beattie had also been a doubt for the Final, a cartilage operation having ruled him out for a large part of the season, and he had been used sparingly by Robson.

Indeed, he appeared in only 21 of Town's 58 competitive matches during the 1977–78 campaign, and was nowhere near 100 per cent fit for the Final. Robson effectively wrapped him in cotton wool to ensure he would play at Wembley.

Beattie said: "I was about 60 per cent fit, but I knew I would not let anyone down. I had two cortisone injections before the game and one at half-time to kill the pain in my knee.

"I am not blaming the boss (he still affectionately referred to Robson as 'Boss' all those years later) or the club – I was prepared to have those injections because I wanted to win the cup for Ipswich."

Beattie said the sight of all the blue and white flags as the teams came out of the tunnel spurred him on that afternoon.

"After the final whistle it was unbelievable. I remember going up the steps and some fans in the crowd were crying with enjoyment.

"Me and Big Al were gagging for a fag and we managed to have a quick puff on the way up."

He recalled the reception that the Ipswich players received from not only their own fans, but the Arsenal fans too, during their lap of honour.

"They called it the 'friendly final' – there was rivalry on the pitch but not off the pitch. It was something you never, ever forget.

"After the game my knee was like a balloon, but I didn't care because we had won the cup. Winning the 1978 FA Cup Final has got to be the greatest day of my life."

Unfortunately for Beattie his persistent knee problems cut short his professional career just as he should have been reaching his prime.

He missed the UEFA Cup Final in 1981 after breaking his arm in the FA Cup semi-final loss to Manchester City at Villa Park less than a month before, and left the club in July 1982.

It was a travesty that a player of his stature won only nine full England caps, and since his career ended he has been dogged by bad luck and misfortune, admittedly some of it self-inflicted.

It was during our interview that Beattie revealed his dying wish – that of having his ashes scattered over his beloved Portman Road – and handed me a back-page story for the *EADT*.

The Carlisle-born defender said he loved Suffolk so much he would never move away from the county.

"I was 15 when I came down here. I have spent so many years here. If it wasn't for the people of Suffolk what would I have done?

"When the big man up there decides that my time has come I want my ashes scattered on Portman Road in the four corners of the ground – north, east, south and west – just to say The Beat is still here."

10. Double Scotch

HE played in a World Cup, a European Cup Final and a UEFA Cup Final.

But John Wark's most memorable team moment in football came at the tender age of 21 when he won the FA Cup with Ipswich Town.

Wark represented Scotland in the 1982 World Cup Finals in Spain, played in the 1985 European Cup Final that Liverpool lost 1–0 to Juventus and was marred by the Heysel tragedy and was, of course, pivotal to Ipswich's 1981 UEFA Cup success, scoring 14 goals en route to Town lifting the trophy.

But all those team achievements are overshadowed by Ipswich's 1–0 FA Cup Final victory over Arsenal at Wembley in 1978.

He said: "Winning the FA Cup gave me a bigger buzz than when we won the UEFA Cup, when we had a better team. I was only 21 when we won the FA Cup, but as a team it rated as the best moment."

It was Wark, the midfielder with an eye for goal, whose header had confirmed Town's place in their first – and so far only – FA Cup Final.

His 90th minute goal in the semi-final against West Bromwich Albion at Highbury eased the nerves and clinched a 3–1 win after Albion had been threatening an equaliser.

He said: "I have scored loads of goals in my career, but that one was the most important.

"It gave me such a buzz because we knew we had done it – we were going to Wembley. That win really put us on the map."

Wark was so nearly Town's match-winner at Wembley, twice

striking the same post – the first from just inside the penalty area and the second from 25 yards – in the second period.

Sitting in The Falcon pub at Rushmere on the outskirts of Ipswich he told me: "Even to this day I thought both shots were going in when I hit them.

"The first one came to me quickly and I hit it as straight as a die and the rebound came back so quickly that Paul Mariner could not direct the rebound into the net.

"The second one Clive Woods laid it back to me and I hit it perfectly and it smacked against the post as Pat Jennings did not move."

Around 20 of Wark's relatives travelled down from his native Glasgow for the Final, and during the lap of honour he spotted his sister at the fence so went over and gave her a hug.

So he was bemused later on when he was met with some glum faces.

He explained: "After the game I went to see my family, but they all looked miserable. I couldn't understand why and so asked them what was up.

"They said 'Why didn't you score?' because they had backed me to score the first goal at 20-1! Typical Jocks!"

Wark admitted his memories of the celebrations that evening were something of a blur, but he had no such problem recalling the journey back to Suffolk on the Sunday.

"We headed down the A12 and stopped at the Army and Navy pub at Chelmsford for a couple of drinks. That just wouldn't be allowed nowadays," he said.

Unlike most ex-pros, Wark continued to play on into his forties and even past his 50th birthday.

He not only turned out on Sundays for Ipswich Licensed Trades League side Sophtlogic, but became manager and chairman of the club as well!

Wark, whose career saw him play in some of the greatest stadiums in the world, said: "We were playing in a game at Chilton Fields in Stowmarket and someone asked: 'Where are the changing rooms?' I had to tell them there weren't any. We had to change in the car.

"I still love it. I may moan a lot, but then I think I am still playing with professionals. I still want to win, even in training."

Wark won 29 Scottish cups, several of them alongside his Ipswich Town team-mate George Burley, who was manager of the national side at the time of the 30th anniversary of Town's cup success.

I had arranged to ring Burley from home, but just a few minutes into our conversation the phone went dead – my two sons had a habit of leaving it off the receiver so that it didn't fully re-charge.

I had to drive back to the office and ring Burley back, but by this time I had missed my slot and so had to re-arrange to call him the following day instead.

Burley enjoyed success at Wembley with Ipswich as both a player and a manager, guiding the club to the Premier League via the 2000 Play-off Final thanks to a thrilling 4–2 victory over Barnsley.

He said: "The whole build-up to the FA Cup Final over the four weeks after the semi-final was tremendous, but as a one-off game as a manager to go up to the Premiership was certainly special."

Burley netted just 11 times in 500 appearances for the club, but his most memorable goal came in the emphatic 6–1 victory in the quarter-final tie at Millwall.

His goal at The Den, sadly, was overshadowed by violence among the home supporters who spilled onto the pitch and caused the match to be held up for 18 minutes while order was restored.

Burley's 30-yard strike – his first goal for 11 months – flew past Nicky Johns to put Ipswich ahead after just ten minutes.

He recalled: "It is the one I remember the most being as it was in the quarter-final of the FA Cup. I didn't get that many and it was one of the best I scored."

Burley so nearly broke the deadlock in the final itself – only a wonder save from Jennings prevented his header from giving Ipswich the lead following a left-wing cross from Woods.

"I met it really well and I could see it was going into the top corner. Pat, who was a great shot-stopper, moved very late and with those big hands of his pawed it away to my disbelief," he recalled.

Bu Ipswich's dominance was eventually rewarded when Roger Osborne scored the only goal of the game in the 78th minute.

Burley said: "Like all the rest of the lads to get to a Cup Final was something you only dreamed about, so to win it was a fantastic feeling."

"After the game everyone was absolutely shattered – we were still shattered the next day," he added.

However, there was a surprise in store for the right-back when he climbed the famous 39 steps as Town went up to collect the cup.

As he was nearing the top of the steps the 21-year-old found himself engulfed by an enthusiastic supporter.

Burley recalled: "I was going up to collect my medal when my mum grabbed me and gave me a big hug!

"She would not let go for what seemed about two minutes. I didn't expect her to be there right at the top of the steps, but it was a great moment for my mum and dad."

11. Basil Brush and Noddy

NOWADAYS players often parade around Wembley after winning the FA Cup Final with their young children.

Back in 1978 Ipswich Town were accompanied on their lap of honour by none other than Basil Brush, the fox glove puppet!

Goalkeeper Paul Cooper can clearly be seen in some of the after-match photographs carrying the popular children's television character.

Cooper recalled: "An old lady who was an Ipswich fan had sent it in as a good luck charm that season.

"It travelled with us along with the kit. I can't remember exactly what happened but I think it was Russell Osman, who was not in the team but sat on the bench, who handed it to me."

Cooper only missed two of Town's 58 games in the 1977–78 season – and one of those came the week before at Aston Villa, after failing a fitness test on a back injury.

Paul Overton was called up for his debut – it turned out to be his one and only first-team appearance – as Ipswich lost 6–1.

That was in stark contrast to seven days later when Cooper was a virtual spectator at Wembley, making only two saves of any note in the entire 90 minutes.

He recalled: "It was a sense of relief more than anything at the final whistle. I was mentally, although not physically, knackered.

"I remember Mick Mills said 'Take in every moment because your career is soon over and you may never be here again.'

"I remember shaking hands with (Arsenal centre-forward)

Malcolm Macdonald afterwards and he was mortified. He had been spouting off before the game what they were going to do to us, but we played well."

Cooper pointed out that although Arsenal were saying beforehand about the injuries they had, the Town team never played together again.

"The big man (Allan Hunter) hardly played after that, Kevin Beattie had lots of injury problems and Roger Osborne had a knee operation and then moved on to Colchester. Before you knew it, the team was being rebuilt for 1981."

Of the 12 players involved in the Cup Final Cooper was the last to leave the club nine years later.

He was the only uncapped player in the side that lifted the UEFA Cup at the end of the 1980–81 campaign, enjoying an outstanding season and winning the club's coveted player of the year trophy.

"I was the only non-international in the side, so whenever they all went away I had a few days playing golf!

"It would have been nice to get a cap, but I was just content to be playing in such a good team on a week by week basis," he said.

Cooper, who joined Ipswich from Birmingham City in March 1974, stayed until after the play-off semi-final, second leg defeat to Charlton Athletic in May 1987. That loss meant Ipswich were destined to spend another season in the old Division Two, and he agreed to sign for Leicester City where former team-mate Bryan Hamilton was manager.

Spells followed at Manchester City and Stockport County, which he described as a real culture shock having played at the top level all his career, before an elbow injury saw him pack up.

He subsequently moved to the sunshine island of Tenerife and set up a business selling tee times online to tour operators and individuals cheaper than they could book themselves.

Brian Talbot, the only Ipswich-born player in the Cup Final squad, also moved abroad after his career finished.

Noddy, as he was nicknamed during his time at Portman Road, ended up living and managing in Malta.

But he kept his house in Brookmans Park, near Potters Bar, the village he moved to when he left Ipswich for £450,000 to join Arsenal in January 1979.

I only had a phone number for his house in Hertfordshire and so left a message on his answerphone.

I was in luck – Talbot returned home soon after, picked up the message and arranged to meet me at The Crown pub in Claydon, just outside Ipswich.

Talbot had played a pivotal role in Town's semi-final win against West Bromwich Albion, even though he was only on the field for seven minutes.

That's how long it took him to open the scoring, but in doing so there was a sickening clash of heads with Albion skipper John Wile.

Both players were left laid out and in urgent need of medical attention; while Wile was bandaged up and carried on, Talbot had suffered a gash just above his right eye.

"It would have been a waste of time if I had been injured and not scored, but fortunately it went in and gave everyone a lift and put us on the road to winning the match," he said.

Talbot was led away to be stitched up and reappeared ten minutes later, but after running up and down the touchline he knew he was not fit to continue and was replaced by substitute Mick Lambert.

He spent most of the remainder of the match in the dressing room trying to sleep, but returned in time to see Town's third goal go in and join in the post-match celebrations.

Even though his eye was closed up and his head was throbbing, Talbot was back in action the following morning in his role as manager of Ipswich Sunday Morning League side Westgate Ward FC.

Being a 'local boy made good' Talbot was in demand when it came to securing Cup Final tickets for family and friends.

He recalled: "I said to Bobby Robson I wanted 54 tickets for the Final to give to family and friends.

"A coachload went to the semi-final, but for the Final, tickets were at a premium. I got a sufficient number but some people were disappointed."

Talbot said he was surprised that Arsenal were such hot favourites to win at Wembley, bearing in mind Ipswich had international players sprinkled throughout their team.

He said Ipswich were still seen as country cousins, even though they had been a very good side under the management of Bobby Robson for several years.

And so it proved. Town's midfield dynamo ran himself into the ground during their triumph before his attentions switched to the homecoming the following day.

He remembered: "From Chelmsford all the way home down the A12 there were supporters on the side of the road, which just showed what it meant to them.

"Sometimes when you are young you do not appreciate the relevance and importance of it all.

"I think too much is made of football – it is not a matter of life and death – but it is important to a lot of people in their lives and when we won the cup it was something which had never happened before – and has not happened since."

Twelve months after winning the cup with Town, Talbot was back at Wembley with Arsenal for the 1979 Final against Manchester United, which the Gunners won 3–2 thanks to a last-gasp winner.

He scored the opening goal, although at the time it was credited to team-mate Alan Sunderland, who later played for Town.

Talbot concluded: "Sundy kicked my boot as I connected with the ball. I don't know if he would have been quite so keen to give the goal to me if he had not scored the winner!"

12. On a wing and a prayer

WEMBLEY winner Clive Woods was almost the one that got away so far as Ipswich Town were concerned.

Woods played in a trial match for Ipswich Reserves against Northampton Town Reserves in 1967, which Town won 2–0.

But it was to be another two years before he was invited back by scout Reg Tyrrell, who watched the winger play for Norwich side Gothic. He appeared in several reserve fixtures before he was invited to sign by manager Bobby Robson.

Woods, who lived in Norwich, didn't own a car then, so walked from his mum's home to the station to catch the train.

Trevor Whymark (who missed out on the 1978 FA Cup Final after injury) would get on at Diss to join him for the journey to Ipswich.

Woods recalled that after defeating Chelsea 3–0 at Portman Road he was having a coffee with Whymark at Ipswich Station while waiting to catch the train back to Norwich.

They were approached by Jack Mansell, the Reading manager at the time, who said 'Would you two like to come to Reading?' and pushed his card into Woods' hand.

However, within a few days both Woods and Whymark got a call from Robson asking them to sign.

Woods, who cost Ipswich £50, recalled: "I was earning £18 a week working in a shoe factory, and I signed for Ipswich on £20 a week, although I got £18 in the summer when I wasn't playing.

"I wanted to become a footballer so much I didn't worry about the money. All I was interested in was playing well and enjoying it."

Woods, who met me at Dunston Hall Hotel not far from his home in Norfolk, said his natural fitness – he used to run virtually every night of the week – helped him adapt to playing professional football.

"Although I was skilful, I had good levels of stamina as well," he continued.

"People love to watch players doing tricks rather than the direct approach of knocking the ball over the top. When I played, people used to like watching Stan Bowles, Rodney Marsh and Tony Currie. They were all flair players who were better than me.

"I could have been as skilful as them, but I was probably more of a team player. It didn't matter if they lost the ball, but if I did I would probably have been dropped!"

Whether Woods was as skilful as Bowles, Marsh and Currie is a matter of opinion, but he certainly turned on the style in the FA Cup Final.

A banner unfurled by Town fans inside Wembley Stadium proclaimed 'Woods fries Rice' – and few would argue that he gave Arsenal right-back Pat Rice the run around that May afternoon.

Woods was the undisputed Man of the Match in the eyes of the majority of the 100,000 inside the stadium and the world-wide television audience.

The silky-skilled left-winger was the catalyst for Town's 1–0 success, but Woods modestly refused to accept he was the best player on view.

He said: "I don't think so. Sometimes you would have games when you had some luck.

"You did not go out to have a bad game – sometimes it would go for you and sometimes it didn't. You are only human in everything you try."

Woods said he believed the underdogs' 1–0 victory was down to their team spirit and their desire to lift the trophy.

At the final whistle he said: "I remember going up to Noddy

(Brian Talbot) and grabbing him and then Millsy (captain Mick Mills) as we celebrated.

"You forget about the opposition and shaking hands because you are so overcome with emotion. Then I remember going up to collect the cup and I was right behind Millsy.

"That moment is the thing most footballers wish for. Some might say winning the league or a European competition is better, but I don't think you can beat winning the cup at Wembley."

Woods, who was selected for one England squad but never played, described winning the FA Cup as the highlight of his career.

After the match Woods quickly changed and went to find his brother Denis, who had played professionally for Cambridge United and Watford, and had flown over from Norway for the Final.

"He wanted to see inside the dressing room, and although he wasn't supposed to be in there with the team, if you look at the photographs of us celebrating afterwards you can see Denis there smoking a cigar!" he said.

Mick Lambert was often competing with Woods for the left-wing berth during his time at Ipswich Town.

But the 1977–78 season had been a frustrating one for Lambert, who had been hampered by a hamstring injury for the majority of the campaign, although he did feature in four of Town's seven FA Cup ties.

He came off the bench (each team back then was only allowed to name one substitute) to replace Brian Talbot, who was injured while scoring just seven minutes into the semi-final against West Bromwich Albion at Highbury.

Three minutes after coming on Lambert had a hand in Town's second goal in their 3–1 win, Albion failing to clear his right-wing corner and Mills pouncing inside the six-yard box to rifle home the loose ball.

Town's victory was all the sweeter for the likes of Lambert, one of several players involved in Town's 2–1 semi-final loss to West Ham United in a replay at Stamford Bridge three years earlier.

Welsh referee Clive Thomas had controversially disallowed not one but two Bryan Hamilton goals that night to dash Ipswich's hopes of a first FA Cup Final appearance.

"We felt we were robbed by Clive Thomas. As far as I remember the linesman never gave offside, but Thomas, who always told everyone he was the best referee around, disallowed both goals.

"I was unsure whether he was right or wrong, but I remember thinking we were robbed," recalled Lambert.

I met Lambert at his Ipswich home only a mile from where I live and during our interview in his kitchen he recalled how the team were convinced they would win the Final.

So much so that several of the Ipswich players placed a bet – now an illegal practice – on Town winning.

Lambert revealed: "Six or seven of us put £20 each on us winning. I rang a bookmaker friend of mine, Alan Monks, and he put the bet on. We got odds of 5-2, so we each won £70 which was a lot of money bearing in mind I was on about £200 a week."

Despite his injury woes Lambert was praying he would be involved in the Final – and he thought the odds were in his favour when boss Bobby Robson left him out of the squad the weekend before.

He explained: "Robson told me to play for the reserves to get my fitness up for the following weekend, which meant I missed the 6–1 debacle at Aston Villa, so I was pretty hopeful.

"Although he had inferred I was going to be the substitute I was never actually told I was the sub. It was only on the morning of the Final when we had a team photograph taken at the hotel that I knew for sure as my name was on one of the chairs."

Lambert said that when the players walked out on to the Wembley turf before the match his legs 'went like jelly' but once he had changed and the teams went out the nerves were forgotten.

The substitute's chance to enter the action came after Roger Osborne was left suffering from exhaustion after giving Town the lead in the 78th minute, but Lambert had no time to warm-up.

He said: "I had been sub a lot of times, so I was used to it. I have seen the Final since and I actually touched the ball more than I thought at the time."

Although he played less than a quarter-of-an-hour, Lambert had no regrets at his bit-part role in Town's victory.

"After the injury problems I had that season I was just grateful to be there, and also to go on in the circumstances I did, replacing Roger who scored what was the winning goal.

"It is better to go on like that than when you are losing 1–0 and you have to try to save the game.

"I probably didn't feel as elated as everyone else afterwards because I had only played 15 minutes, but I was pleased for everyone around me," he said.

13. The unlikely lads

ROGER Osborne was the most unlikely of Wembley match-winners.

But a week before the FA Cup Final he thought his chance of playing in the showpiece occasion had gone when he was dropped from the team for Ipswich Town's final league game of the season.

Osborne admitted that he was 'devastated and shocked' at being dropped for the match at Villa Park – and so were other players in the team.

His place in the team was taken by South African-born midfielder Colin Viljoen, who like so many of the Town squad, had suffered injury problems over the course of the season.

Manager Bobby Robson was keen to see if he could accommodate Viljoen, who was twice capped by England, in his Wembley line-up.

Osborne, who I interviewed at the *EADT* offices, recalled: "I had organised tickets for all my family – they were coming from Cornwall, Devon and Birmingham – and all of a sudden it was rushing through my head that I was not going to be playing at Wembley."

However, Osborne need not have worried – Ipswich lost 6–1 to Aston Villa and he knew straightaway that he would be restored to the team for the Cup Final.

"I was a popular player and no-one wanted me to be left out. John Wark and Brian Talbot were both moved to accommodate Colin, but it just did not work," he said.

Osborne, who came from a family of six brothers and six sisters, said he was never actually told he would be starting against Arsenal.

He recalled: "Bobby, to be fair, said the only one to come out of the game with any credit was me, so he was saying in a way I was in the team.

"Then in training during the week prior to the Cup Final everyone knew who was doing what and it became quite obvious that I was in the team."

On the day of the Final itself Osborne said a walk on the Wembley pitch prior to kick-off helped Ipswich to overcome any Pre-Cup Final nerves.

He described the noise as they emerged from the tunnel in their Cup Final suits as 'unbelievable' before then spending 20 minutes on the pitch trying to take it all in.

"If we hadn't gone out at two o'clock and instead gone out at ten to three, then it would have been mind-blowing, but by going out on the pitch at two o'clock we got acclimatised to what was going to happen."

Osborne's role was to mark Arsenal's talented midfield playmaker Liam Brady, who he kept quiet during the course of the afternoon.

But few people would have backed Osborne to score the most famous goal in the club's history.

After all, he only scored a total of ten goals in 127 appearances for Ipswich plus a further 22 outings as a substitute.

But when Arsenal defender Willie Young could only deflect a hard, low cross from David Geddis into his path, Osborne pounced by drilling the ball past Pat Jennings.

He explained: "The only thing I can remember at the time was concentrating on keeping the ball low. It was not a question of trying to find the corner of the goal as I was only eight, nine or ten yards out. It was a question of just trying to hit the target."

And hit the target he did, before being engulfed by team-mates jumping on top of him in the euphoria that followed Ipswich finally breaching Arsenal's defence.

When the celebrations died down Osborne was left feeling faint

– it was very humid inside the stadium as it had rained on the morning of the match before the sun came out.

"What with the heat and people jumping on top of me and the fact I had scored, I was overcome. There was no other reason for it. It wasn't a case of I couldn't carry on.

"I have always said if there wasn't such a thing as substitutes and they gave me two or three minutes to recover I would have carried on," he added.

Osborne was replaced by Mick Lambert and spent the next 15 minutes sitting on the Town bench before Town's victory was confirmed.

"The final whistle, obviously apart from personal things like getting married and having my boys, has got to be the pinnacle of my life," he explained.

Osborne acquired celebrity status overnight and was in big demand that summer as he was invited to open countless fetes.

However, a knee injury he had been struggling with before the Final required an operation, and he suffered an infection after open surgery.

He did not play in a single first-team game the following season and made just four starts plus a further two as a substitute in the 1979–80 campaign before being sold to Colchester United for £25,000 in February 1981.

Geddis, who set up Osborne's winner, left Portman Road even sooner, signing for Aston Villa for £300,000 in September 1979.

An FA Cup winner at the age of just 20, Geddis appeared to have the world at his feet at the club.

However, within just a few months his life was turned upside down when he was involved in a car accident which claimed the life of close friend Peter Canavan.

Not only was Canavan an Ipswich team-mate but a promising defender who had already represented England at under-17 level.

But it was the emergence of Alan Brazil, who netted nine league goals in just 14 starts and a further five substitute appearances, during the 1978–79 season that led to Geddis leaving.

Geddis didn't want to be just a squad player so agreed to move to Villa, where he had played the week before the Cup Final alongside Trevor Whymark, who had not long returned to action after straining knee ligaments on Boxing Day.

Geddis himself had missed the semi-final against West Bromwich Albion with a groin strain, with Robin Turner playing in his place.

Now Bobby Robson challenged Geddis and Whymark to fight for the right to wear the jersey at Wembley the following week.

Geddis said: "Trevor had played a couple of games leading up to the Final. He was a fantastic centre-forward. There were not many better that I have come across in my playing and coaching career, so when we were pitched together as a pairing at Aston Villa the week before the Final, I thought there was more of a chance of me missing out."

Geddis, who I interviewed over the phone at his home in his native north-east, said he thought he would be the one left out following Town's dismal 6–1 drubbing that day.

It was not until the following Thursday that he was told he would be in the team for the Final, with both Whymark and Turner missing out altogether.

Geddis was deployed wide on the right with Clive Woods on the left, leaving Paul Mariner to plough a lone furrow through the middle in the final.

The aim was to stop Arsenal full-backs Pat Rice and Sammy Nelson getting forward. It proved to be a masterstroke – not only did the plan achieve that, but Geddis also set up the winning goal.

"I can't describe it. I guess if you are an amateur player who loves playing football and you score a goal, that is the closest you are going to get to it. It was as though I had scored myself," explained Geddis.

In the aftermath of the celebrations it was not only Osborne who was struggling.

Geddis recalled: "It was a very hot day – the temperature was up to 85 – and I was suffering from dehydration. It was so hot inside the stadium that I had sunburnt hands and arms because I wore a short-sleeved shirt."

He recovered sufficiently to stay on the field until the final whistle blew.

"The only way you can imagine it, is anyone playing at the height of their profession and achieving their goal and to times it by ten," he concluded.

14. Leading from the front

MICK Mills was so upset by his side's semi-final defeat he could not face watching the 1975 FA Cup Final.

Such was the pain of the controversial 2–1 replay defeat to West Ham United at Stamford Bridge that the Ipswich Town skipper could not stomach seeing the Wembley showpiece on television.

He recalled: "I think 1975 was the only Cup Final I have not watched since 1955 – I went racing at Newmarket instead.

"I haven't got a clue what happened – I stayed well away from it. I was that gutted at not being there I could not watch it. I was still hungover from the semi-final defeat when the Final was played."

As captain and the only person to ever lift the FA Cup in the club's history, I was especially looking forward to interviewing Mills.

We met in the media suite at Portman Road two hours before a home midweek match against Sheffield United in March 2008.

Mills has always been an excellent talker, and he gave me enough material to write not one but two double-page features.

As well as the article I was preparing on each player, I wrote a separate piece that appeared on 6 May – 30 years on from the day of the Fnal itself – on Town's round-by-round progress through his eyes.

If you believe in superstitions then a change of room-mates on the eve of the third round was one of those quirks of fate that contributed to Town winning the trophy.

Mills and Allan Hunter roomed together before the tie at Cardiff, and following Town's 2–0 victory they teamed up on away trips for the rest of the competition all the way to Wembley.

"Allan Hunter was Kevin Beattie's big mate and they always shared a room, but Kevin was not playing and so Allan and I roomed together at Cardiff," explained Mills.

"We said as we had never been thrown together before, this might be a superstitious thing that we have to keep going, and so we did. We didn't have many away ties, but when we did we roomed together right up to the Final."

Mills was convinced of the fact that nine of the side had been involved in that heartbreaking semi-final defeat in 1975 was a defining factor in Ipswich winning the cup three years later.

The only three of the Wembley line-up that had not been a part of the side in 1975 were goalkeeper Paul Cooper, who was at the club but understudy to Laurie Sivell, David Geddis and Paul Mariner.

Mills said there was no comparison to what the 1975 side achieved and the winning team of 1978.

"When you consider the teams that we beat in '75 and the fact we played nine games in total, we should have won the cup and we never even got to the Final!

"That year included four games against Leeds United, who were the best club side I have ever played against, which should give you the trophy on its own, then we had two matches against West Ham.

"In '78 we only played seven games – West Brom and then Arsenal were the only First Division sides we met – and we won it," he explained.

Mills said a string of injuries that season led to the club's most inconsistent run of results over a ten-year period, which meant Ipswich were languishing at the wrong end of the table.

But they came good in the FA Cup, and belied their status as underdogs to beat West Brom 3–1 in the semi-final to reach the Final.

He recalled that when the final whistle blew at Wembley his first thought was to share the moment with as many of his team-mates as he could, before trying to acknowledge family and friends in the stands.

Mills said: "It was in the back of my mind all the time that I was going to be collecting the cup. It was the most wonderful feeling ever in football.

"We started going up the 39 steps to the Royal Box but after about eight or nine steps I disappeared under a forest of arms and bodies and could not see anything because of all the well-wishers leaning over patting me on the back, until all of a sudden I got to a point where the fans could not reach me any more."

Mills, who won 42 full England caps and captained his country at the 1982 World Cup Finals in Spain, then stopped, drew breath and looked around him.

As he prepared to receive the famous old trophy from Princess Alexandra, he recalled: "It is at this point that it hit me. I could see the royalty, our chairman Patrick Cobbold and the trophy, as well as the fans all around the stadium. It was definitely the best moment of my career."

While Mills led from the front as captain, England team-mate Mariner led the front line for Ipswich at Wembley. And for the striker who had been playing non-league football for Chorley just five years earlier, winning the FA Cup was the realisation of a schoolboy dream.

It was Mariner who had set Ipswich on the way to glory with both goals in the 2–0 third round win at Cardiff City in early January.

He was then on target in each of the next three rounds – one against Hartlepool and Bristol Rovers, before netting a hat-trick in the sixth-round success at Millwall.

Mariner said that Millwall were a very tough team to play against in those days at The Den, and Ipswich were anxious about going there.

He said: "They had a very partisan crowd, but we came out of the blocks very fast, playing our usual style, and George (Burley) scored an absolute screamer.

"I think that took the wind out of their sails and I remember we steamrollered them."

Mariner had just started his fourth season as assistant coach to former Liverpool and Scotland defender Steve Nicol at New England Revolution when we spoke.

It may have been early morning in America when I rang him, but the memories of that afternoon in May 1978 soon came flooding back.

Mariner vividly recalled his feelings as the two teams took to the pitch beneath the twin towers.

"As we came out of the tunnel I remember looking round and seeing all our supporters behind us. I am getting goose pimples just thinking about it now.

"The hairs on the back of my neck stood up as I saw all our fans in blue and white behind us with their scarves and banners, and it gave us such a lift. It was incredible."

Mariner had a great chance to open the scoring as early as the 11th minute, but his shot smacked against the crossbar, after Roger Osborne could only divert a Clive Woods cross into his path.

"In hindsight maybe I should have done better, but it came so quickly to me – the Wembley pitch was like greased lightning. I was a split second slow in reacting and was off balance and it hit the bar. I would have loved to have scored," he said.

Mariner said that although he imagined on the bench and in the stands everyone was thinking Arsenal could break away and score, the Town players out on the pitch always felt they would win.

However, his memory of what happened in the aftermath of victory was rather more hazy.

He said: "I don't really remember what happened at the final whistle. You don't rehearse that moment. I am guessing that I was looking for my mates to give them a hug.

"We were a close-knit group of players. I arrived in 1976 and roomed with Warky for eight years and with Millsy (Mick Mills) for six years with the national team. We were blood brothers so to speak.

"Hunter and Beattie would have wanted to get back to the dressing room for a cigarette and the rest of us could not wait for a beer!"

Mariner admitted he was not feeling too sharp the next morning for the journey back to Ipswich.

"The whole experience was absolutely amazing. It was the first trophy I had won in English football. Everyone who plays football as a kid wants to win the FA Cup, and to do it with that bunch of lads was extremely special in my life and in my football career.

"It was right up there with playing for my country at Wembley and winning the UEFA Cup with a very special team," he added.

Part Four
– Telling tales

15. Game-changer

ESSEX all-rounder Graham Napier told me that he had no regrets at all about turning down the chance to join Ipswich Town as a goalkeeper.

Colchester-born Napier started playing for Ipswich as a 14-year-old schoolboy, and was subsequently offered apprenticeship terms.

Speaking in the summer of 2010 Napier said: "I made the choice to play cricket and do a similar YTS scheme with Essex, but Ipswich said I could carry on playing in their Youth team and continue training."

He trained with Richard Wright and Craig Forrest, Ipswich Town's two recognised senior 'keepers, and the club's goalkeeping coach on a Friday morning, and also with his own age group in midweek.

"I played quite a few Youth team games when they needed me and it was a great experience playing at a professional football club at that level.

"I eventually played one reserve team game, I think against Luton when I was 16, so I stood out as a young goalkeeper effectively in a men's game."

Ipswich fixed up Napier to play one season for Felixstowe Port & Town (now Felixstowe & Walton United) in the Jewson League Premier Division, but he then packed up.

"I have no regrets at all – cricket has taken me all round the world and I have been playing professionally for nearly 14 seasons.

"I didn't see a future for me in football – I am 5 foot 10 inches if I am lucky and there are probably only one or two goalkeepers of that height who have been world-class, but these days you have to be six-foot plus, so I would have struggled.

"Looking at the attributes you need to be a goalkeeper, I had the agility but not the height."

It is not surprising that Napier has no regrets about the career path he chose.

He has enjoyed a successful career as a county cricketer and on the evening of 24 June 2008 he became the talk of the whole country and beyond.

Essex Eagles were hosting the Sussex Sharks in a Twenty20 group game that was being televised live on Sky TV.

Napier walked to the wicket at the Ford County Ground in Chelmsford with Essex 13 for one in the second over of their innings.

Nineteen overs later he walked off after scoring an incredible 152 not out off only 58 deliveries.

Napier re-wrote the record books on that balmy summer's night, smashing 16 sixes – the highest in an individual Twenty20 innings – as well as scoring the most runs in boundaries (136 – ten fours and 16 sixes) in an individual Twenty20 innings.

His knock also broke the record for the most sixes in a domestic one-day innings, and tied the record set by Australian Andrew Symonds for most sixes in a domestic innings which he set in a county championship match in 1995.

I was interested to find out how that innings had changed the life of the former Colchester & East Essex all-rounder, who said he considered himself a bowler first even though he enjoyed batting more.

"My life has changed dramatically. Two years ago, before that game against Sussex, I had application forms for the police and fire brigade and was seriously considering filling them out and seeing where it took me," he said.

"However, it wasn't just the one game – I had a consistent run of form during the season that got me an IPL contract with Mumbai Indians and also a contract to play in New Zealand as an overseas professional with Central Districts."

Napier explained that such contracts were normally only ever given to international players, and it was a great honour for him.

He had enjoyed two successful winters in New Zealand, culminating in winning the Twenty20 competition the previous winter, before going back out to the IPL earlier that year.

"So in those terms, my career has gone from almost considering life outside of cricket and probably finishing my career early, to a position where I have had two wonderful years playing cricket and I hope for a few more."

Following on from his record-breaking innings and a successful summer, Napier was selected in the England squad for the ICC World Twenty20 held in this country the following year.

But he never made the actual team, even though England had a poor tournament.

He was subsequently overlooked in 2010 for the competition in the West Indies, which saw England record their first success in any ICC world event in 35 years.

However, he was in no mood to throw in the towel so far as his chances of representing his country were concerned.

"My hopes of playing for England won't go until I retire from cricket full stop. Everyone still dreams of pulling on an England shirt whether it is the first day of your professional career or the last," he said.

At least he had played in the IPL, and even though he had only appeared in one IPL match in two years, Napier had revelled in the experience, the riches and razzmatazz being a far cry from the daily grind of county cricket in front of a few hundred spectators.

"It is a big show – and that is probably the best way to describe it. It is about entertainment and the cricket is the most important part of that, but to be in a position to sit alongside Sachin Tendulkar, Zaheer Khan, J.P. Duminy, Sanath Jayasuriya, Kieron Pollard – the list is almost endless – and train with these guys, talk cricket and talk tactics with them, has been a great learning experience for me."

Napier felt that the absence of the words 'international cricketer' from his CV may have counted against him when it came to selecting the Mumbai team, but said it had still been phenomenal to be involved.

He added: "To be one of only eight out of a professional pool of 400 players in England puts you right up there with the top names.

"The highlight for me was that at one point in the winter I was the leading wicket-taker in the world in Twenty20 cricket, which shows that I am not just a batsman, but a bowler as well."

It was to be nearly three more years before Napier's record of most sixes in an innings was broken by none other than Chris Gayle while playing for Bangalore Royal Challengers in the IPL.

The West Indian opening batsman smashed 17 sixes and 13 fours on his way to an unbeaten 175 from only 66 balls against Pune Warriors – the highest individual score in the IPL.

I rang Napier that afternoon in April 2013 to get his reaction to his record finally being taken away from him.

He revealed that the Essex squad had delayed their afternoon training session by 15 minutes to see the end of Gayle's innings and see him break the record.

Napier admitted: "I am a bit gutted about that, but records are made to be broken. I knew it would happen at some point and he was the one most likely to do it.

"He is a class act, especially at that form of the game and he brings a lot to the game with his cool persona and his ability to smash the ball around the park."

He said that with the sheer volume of T20 cricket being played around the globe he thought the record would have previously been broken and that it was only a matter of time before it fell.

Napier added: "They will have to change it to 'former world record holder' when talking about me!"

16. Record breakers

JUST as the BBC has *EastEnders* and ITV has *Coronation Street*, so Suffolk cricket had its own long-running soap opera.

It centred on whether Phil Caley would finally become Suffolk's leading all-time run scorer.

A year after the record first started to loom on the horizon, Caley finally achieved the milestone after a run of low scores and missed opportunities. Caley, who made his debut for Suffolk in 1982, scored the last six runs he required against Hertfordshire in June 2009, to finally pass the 9,219 aggregate in the Minor Counties Championship achieved by Clements.

The left-handed Clements, like Caley a former Ipswich School pupil, passed Tony Warrington's total of 7,623 in July 1993, during the second innings of Suffolk's game against Buckinghamshire at Copdock.

I remember interviewing Clements after that innings to find out what it meant to him to break the record and, typically of Clements, he replied: "What was the record anyway?" But for Caley the record had become a millstone around his neck, after it became clear he was closing in on his former team-mate.

He appeared certain to reach the landmark the previous season – his final summer in charge after 15 years at the helm as county captain – when he required just 16 runs with three matches remaining. However, he made three and three away to Northumberland, four and did not bat at Norfolk and did not even get to the wicket in the final match of the season at home to Hertfordshire!

There was no certainty that he would retain his place in the side the following season, after being virtually ever-present for an incredible 27 years.

Caley had missed just two championship matches during his entire career – one because he could not get the whole two days off work (he ended up watching for a day-and-a-half instead!) and the other when he was suffering from Quinsies, a severe throat infection.

But he was given the opportunity to carry on the following season, even though Justin Bishop was then skipper and Caley was aged 46 when the season started.

Even then he was made to wait, again failing to get to the crease to bat in either innings even though he was listed to go in at No.6 in the season's opening game against Bedfordshire.

It looked as though Caley was going to have to wait a while longer when Martyn Cull became the first Suffolk batsman since 1911 to register a double century and Hassan Adnan scored a ton in a third wicket stand of 223 against Hertfordshire at Hertford.

But Caley's chance came at the fall of Suffolk's fourth wicket and he finished on 37 not out to eclipse Clements' record.

Caley reflected: "It was a shame I didn't get the record in the final game of last season at Bury St Edmunds, because we took 19 Hertfordshire wickets and they only got two of ours and I didn't even get my pads on for three days which was disappointing.

"It was a home game and it would have been nice to have done it there, and it didn't happen in the opening match at home to Bedfordshire when we only lost six wickets and again I didn't get into bat.

"But it is a nice achievement for me, although it is not the be all and end all."

Fast forward two years and Adnan broke a 100-year-old record himself, although he later admitted he did not know it at the time.

The former Derbyshire batsman surpassed the individual highest score by a Suffolk batsman of 229 set by J.F. Ireland against Cambridgeshire at Newmarket.

Adnan finished on 232 not out at the end of the second day of Suffolk's Minor Counties Championship match against Northumberland at Jesmond.

His innings was also confirmed as the highest in the Eastern Division – the championship had been split into two divisions in 1983 – trumping the 226 not out by Norfolk's Carl Amos at Lakenham in 1998 versus Lincolnshire.

I rang skipper Bishop on his mobile phone the following morning when I knew the Suffolk players would be having breakfast in their hotel, and he put Adnan on to speak to me.

The softly-spoken Pakistan-born batsman, whose highest first-class score was 191 against Somerset at Taunton in 2005, told me: "It is certainly the best innings I have ever played.

"I had no idea I had broken the individual batting record, so I was surprised and very happy to be told that I had done so.

"I was also very happy when our scorer (Andy Broome) told me that I had set a new record for the Eastern Division and also that it was a fifth-wicket record for Suffolk as well."

Suffolk batted on for a further five overs that morning as Adnan ended undefeated on 236 and partner Chris Warn 115 not out as they extended their stand to 293 – just two runs shy of the county's all-time record for any wicket – to set up a 328-run victory.

The Catley brothers set a record of a different type in June 1999 when Matthew and Tim were selected for their debuts against Bedfordshire alongside older brother Russell.

The match at Bedford Town CC marked the first time in Suffolk's history that three brothers had represented the county.

It was also believed to be the first time the feat had been achieved anywhere in Minor Counties cricket since World War Two.

Matthew, 24, and 21-year-old Tim played for Exning alongside

Russell, who was 26 and First XI captain. Father Tony was club secretary and club captain just for good measure.

Russell said: "Me, Matt and Tim take up three of the top four batting positions and dad runs the club, which people call 'Catley CC'.

"It will be a proud moment for our parents, who will be watching, and hopefully they won't cramp our style and we won't cramp theirs too much! We are all really looking forward to it."

Ipswich Town legend Ted Phillips was also a more than useful cricketer and took 24 wickets in just six matches for Suffolk after making his debut in 1965.

Phillips, who was renowned for having the hardest shot in the game, scored 161 goals in 269 appearances for the club, and together with Ray Crawford played a pivotal role in Ipswich winning the old First Division Championship in 1961–62.

What is not so well known is that for 45 years he held the record for the best bowling figures for Colchester & East Essex Cricket Club.

The former Ipswich striker recorded figures of 18.3-14-5-9 against Clacton at Castle Park in 1967.

That was the same season that he set a Colchester & East Essex club record of 143 wickets at an average of just 11.06.

But that record was shattered in May 2012 when Gareth Fisher claimed nine wickets for only four runs as Woodford Wells were dismissed for just 24 in the Shepherd Neame Essex Premier League.

That summer coincided with the 150th anniversary of the club, who over the years have boasted some top-class players who have also played for Essex.

These include ex-England trio Neil Foster, Derek Pringle and Peter Such and all-rounders Graham Napier, Adam Seymour, Nadeem Shahid and John Stephenson.

There was no sign of the drama that was about to unfold when Woodford Wells, after winning the toss and electing to bat, took ten runs off the first over.

Fisher, aged 22 at the time, then produced his devastating spell that included a hat-trick of lbw decisions which then became four wickets in four balls.

The hat-trick was actually the third of Fisher's career, and the four runs he conceded included three wides and only one run off the bat – and that was a dropped catch!

Fisher said afterwards: "I had no idea at all about the record. It was only afterwards that I was told it was a new club record.

"It was an amazing feeling. I joked to (team-mate) Julian Russell that I was thinking of retiring straight away!"

I arranged for Fisher to meet Phillips and be photographed together at Castle Park, scene of both their outstanding performances, for my weekly 'Love Cricket' column in the *EADT* and *Ipswich Star*.

Phillips, who at the time was 78, said: "Records are there to be broken at some stage, so I would like to pat him on the back and say well bowled."

They were photographed with Fisher holding the ball that he wreaked havoc among the Woodford Wells batsmen with.

Phillips said he was never presented with the match ball following his feat and recalled: "I think one of the Clacton players took it home and I never saw it again!"

17. Up for the Cup

UPSETTING your employer is not usually considered a good career move.

So Andy Crump was expecting to cop some flak at work after knocking Ipswich Town out of the Suffolk FA Premier Cup.

Crump, who worked at Portman Road for the Prince's Trust, netted the winner for Felixstowe & Walton United against Ipswich Town in January 2013.

A bumper crowd of 1,050 assembled at the Goldstar Ground to see the Thurlow Nunn League Premier Division side take on a youthful Town team at the competition's quarter-final stage.

Arran Sheppard headed the non-league side ahead after just eight minutes, before Crump volleyed home the second following a corner after 57 minutes.

Although Josh Carson scored direct from a free-kick in the 90th minute it was too little, too late for Town.

Crump, still standing in the middle of the pitch after the match, told me: "I hope I escape any flak that may be coming my way!"

Although a Manchester United supporter and not an Ipswich Town fan, the 27-year-old added: "Because I work at the club I follow them closely, and I have done for a long time, but it is nice to get one over them!"

However, Crump and the Seasiders' joy turned to heartbreak when they were subsequently removed from the competition, after it emerged they had fielded an ineligible player.

Alan Mills cast aside heartbreak of a different kind to score the winner for Whitton United after coming off the bench in the Suffolk FA Senior Cup Final.

Mills scored with a low 20-yard drive that squirmed beneath the dive of Long Melford goalkeeper Paul Wood in the 89th minute of the Final.

His last-gasp goal gave the holders a come-from-behind 2–1 victory at Portman Road in May 2012.

Whitton had drawn level just three minutes before Mills was introduced as a 69th minute substitute.

Mills, who was due to turn 36 the following week, had missed Whitton's 1–0 loss to Godmanchester in the Ridgeons League Division One KO Cup Final just five days before.

But he was fit enough to return to the squad for the Senior Cup Final, only to be left on the bench by boss Ian Brown.

Mills said: "I was heartbroken not to start, even though I could not play on Friday due to injury. I was very disappointed to be left out, and I would be lying if I said I was not."

A runner-up with Ipswich Athletic in the 2000–01 Final against Kirkley, match-winner Mills added: "It is an absolutely brilliant feeling. I have played for a long time but never won this competition before."

Another left-back who was just as unlikely a winning goalscorer was Mark Coulson when Bury Town lifted the Ryman League Cup just two months before in March 2012.

Coulson, who had not scored since October 2010, fired home a 30-yard rocket against fellow Premier Division outfit East Thurrock United for the only goal of the game at Staines Town's ground.

Coulson afterwards admitted: "I don't know where that came from really. I have been waiting a year and a half since scoring against Staines last season in the FA Cup. Sometimes you hit them and you know they are going in."

Another FA Cup hero was Stuart Boardley, who scored twice to fire Leiston to a 3–1 victory over Lewes in a fourth qualifying round replay in October 2008.

It was the first time that Leiston had reached the first round proper of the competition in the club's 127-year history, after sensationally dumping out the Blue Square Premier side.

Leiston, who were playing in the Ridgeons League Premier Division at the time, were the lowest-ranked side left in the competition, but caused an upset as they won the replay at the Dripping Pan.

I tracked down Boardley, who was back behind his desk working as a trainee quantity surveyor for Ipswich firm Brooks & Wood, early the following morning, to speak to him for a back-page story in that day's edition of the *Ipswich Star*.

The 23-year-old revealed that none of his family were present to watch him play after his 80-year-old grandad was taken into hospital earlier in the day.

He said: "He is very ill. He was at the match on Saturday and would have loved to have been there last night. I am quite sad that he was not able to be there, but hopefully he will have heard how we got on and it will lift his spirits."

Boardley, who spent ten years with Ipswich Town as a youngster but never made it to the first-team squad, described the win as the best moment of his career.

Playing in the FA Vase Final for Sudbury Town provided Paul Smith with the best and worst moments of a distinguished career in non-league football.

Smith, one of the best players Suffolk has produced in the past 30 years who has not gone on to make the grade as a professional, was a member of the Sudbury side that faced Tamworth in the final at Wembley Stadium in 1989.

The match finished in a 1–1 draw, with Tamworth winning the replay 3–0 at Peterborough United's London Road ground four days later.

Sudbury were trailing 1–0 in the replay when they were awarded a penalty, which Smith skied over the crossbar.

Casting his mind back to the final ahead of a 20th anniversary reunion, Smith said: "Missing the penalty was the worst moment of my career, and people still talk to me about it!

"Nigel Barton was our regular penalty taker, but he had gone off a few minutes earlier. I felt confident about scoring because I had been taking them while he had been out of the team injured."

Smith, who went on to manage Walsham-le-Willows, said: "I guess I just leant back at the wrong time as I tried to side foot it to the 'keeper's left and got under the ball too much.

"Whether it would have changed the course of the game we will never know, but it took me a long time to get over it."

Cricketer Hedley Wright came close to being an unlikely hero when he almost bowled Suffolk to a memorable cup upset in June 1989.

The all-rounder, who had just turned 36, dismissed England internationals Wayne Larkins, Rob Bailey and Geoff Cook, to leave Northamptonshire 16 for 3 in the first round of the NatWest Trophy.

Wright, playing on his home ground at Bury St Edmunds, had national newspaper reporters ringing their sports editors in a frenzy as they sensed a giant-killing act.

Upsets in the country's premier knockout competition had been few and far between over the years, but Northants had lost to another Minor County, Cheshire, the previous season.

Wright sent shockwaves through the first-class county's dressing room when he claimed three wickets inside the opening five overs of the match at the Victory Ground.

I caught up with Wright on the eve of the two counties meeting in the same competition, then known as the Cheltenham & Gloucester Trophy, at the same venue 13 years later.

Speaking from his High Wycombe home, Wright modestly said:

"I do remember the day quite clearly. Wayne Larkins was somewhat unfortunate.

"I benefited from a lack of paint on the sightscreen as he missed a full toss! I let go of the ball and an expletive at the same time when I realised it was a full toss, but he obviously didn't pick up the flight of the ball and played across it.

"Rob Bailey tried to drive a big inswinger and was beaten by a lack of pace. I think he was expecting it to come through much more rapidly than it did.

"Geoff Cook's dismissal was much the same, he was bowled playing the same shot to the same type of ball.

"But my big regret was that after the third wicket Allan Lamb came in to bat and he nicked his very first delivery past leg stump and all the way to the boundary. That was extremely close to being 16 for 4."

Lamb survived and went on to score 103, putting on 167 for the fourth wicket with fellow England international David Capel, who ended undefeated on 92.

They enabled Northants, whose bowling attack included legendary West Indian paceman Curtly Ambrose, to reach a respectable total of 256 for 4 and provide the platform for an eventual 32-run success.

Alongside that article appeared my interview with South African international Andrew Hall, who was playing as Suffolk's permitted overseas player against Northants in the Third Round of the C&G Trophy just two days later.

Hall had made his Test debut less than three months before against an Australian side containing household names such as Shane Warne, Glenn McGrath and Steve Waugh.

But he admitted he had never heard of the likes of captain Phil Caley and opening batsman Russell Catley, let alone met them!

Hall, who was in England playing as professional at Lancashire side Lytham St Annes, was certainly up for the cup and agreed it was an opportunity to put himself in the shop window.

"I like to play in matches like this one because I want to play county cricket in the future, so it is a good opportunity for me to show what I can do," he told me.

Hall certainly showed what he was capable of and almost helped his Suffolk team-mates upset the odds in that match in May 2002.

Indeed, had it not been for former Essex seam bowler Darren Cousins, who lived in the West Suffolk town of Haverhill, the Minor County would almost certainly have won.

He had opened the bowling for the visitors and returned figures of 8-5-12-2 as Suffolk mustered 128 for nine in their allotted 50 overs.

Cousins, who was not noted for his batting ability, then scored 17 not out to ensure a nail-biting one-wicket win at the Victory Ground in Bury St Edmunds.

The target appeared to be meat and drink to the first-class county as Michael Hussey, who went on to play 79 Tests and 185 one-day internationals for Australia, and Mal Loye rattled up 46 from the opening eight overs.

A rain break and inspired bowling spells by Hall (four for 33) and veteran Clacton seamer Gary Kirk (three for 16) hauled Suffolk back into the match, but even at 91 for 3 the visitors were still in the driving seat.

But when Northants then slipped to 104 for 8, Suffolk looked all set to claim the scalp of the first-class county.

When the ninth wicket fell Cousins, batting at No.10, was joined by last man Jason Brown with two runs still required. Cousins struck the winning boundary much to the relief of his team-mates.

Cousins said afterwards: "All credit to Suffolk, they worked really hard. It was their Cup Final – ten more runs or even one more run and they could have won it."

Despite his contribution with bat and ball the Man of the Match medallion and £325 cheque went to Suffolk's Kevin Shaw, who didn't even know he was playing until 15 minutes before the start!

The Bury St Edmunds all-rounder, batting at No.9, had scored 34 not out and then removed the obdurate Russell Warren for 21 in his only over.

He said: "I am delighted to win the award but it is tinged with disappointment as we were so close to winning and these chances don't come along very often."

Hall meanwhile reflected: "We can be proud of our performance, especially with only 128 runs on the board and then when they reached 91 for 3, but we really pulled it back.

"They probably expected to roll us over and thought they were going to walk it, but we showed that Minor Counties can play in this competition."

Hall clearly made a big impression on Northants, who he joined in 2008 and skippered between 2010 and 2012, before being released two years later.

18. They think it's all over...

PENALTY shoot-outs are often high on drama, but few can match that between two Suffolk & Ipswich League sides in the 2012–13 season.

Melton St Audry's defeated Stanton 14–13 in a fourth-round tie in the Bob Coleman Cup.

The shoot-out consisted of a total of 32 penalties before the sides could be separated.

Melton manager Steve Moore admitted he had stopped watching by the time his goalkeeper, Callum Deacon, made the winning save.

Moore told me: "I had my back turned at that point, but I was told Matt Musgrove hit the penalty straight down the middle and Callum saved it."

With the sides locked at 4–4 after their first five spot kicks, the 25-year-old 'keeper took Melton's first sudden-death spot kick and missed, before atoning by saving Stanton's next attempt. Moore added: "People were texting me afterwards to check what they had heard was right because they did not believe what had happened."

Supporters of both sides could similarly scarcely believe what they witnessed following the breathtaking, see-saw conclusion to the Suffolk FA Senior Cup Final in May 2013.

The match at Portman Road was to be Ipswich Wanderers goalkeeper Jamie Stannard's last appearance before bringing the curtain down on his career.

His only previous appearance in a Cup Final at Portman Road had ended in Leiston's 5–4 defeat on penalties to Needham Market, after a goalless draw in the 2008 Suffolk FA Premier Cup.

The 33-year-old told me before the Final: "At the end I guess it will hit me that my career is over, so it will be nice to stand back and look around Portman Road and think this is where it ends."

It certainly looked all over for Stannard and Wanderers, after Whitton United goalkeeper Liam Jones saved their first three penalties in a shoot-out following a 1–1 draw after extra-time.

Cometh the hour, cometh the man as Stannard, anxious to avoid ending his career with another runners-up medal after a shoot-out defeat, stepped up to the plate.

He saved Whitton's next three penalties to keep his side's slim hopes alive, the third of which from opposing 'keeper Jones would have won the cup for Whitton had he scored.

Dan Tredway netted his spot kick to take it to sudden-death, and then Stannard remarkably saved a fourth successive penalty, this time from Ryan Flynn, before Luke Read converted to win the shoot-out 3–2 for Wanderers.

Stannard said afterwards: "A lot of people said beforehand it would go to penalties because they thought it would be so tight.

"I had everyone saying to me it was written in the stars that we would win, but I thought it was going to be déjà vu because Liam (Jones) was in goal as well the last time, and it got to the point where I had to save a penalty and fortunately I went the right way and then we had to score.

"It is an amazing feeling – this is up there with the best nights of my life in footballing terms, which includes playing in the first round proper of the FA Cup. What this group of lads have achieved is amazing."

Perhaps Stannard couldn't believe it was all over – he subsequently came out of retirement in the 2014–15 season to play for Felixstowe & Walton United.

If Whitton were left shell-shocked, so too were Easton's cricketers when their undefeated start to the season in the summer of 2000 came to a shuddering halt.

The village side from near Framlingham in Suffolk had secured ten straight wins to sit proudly top of the Division Three table in their first season in the Two Counties Championship.

With only four fixtures still to fulfil, Easton were even dreaming of becoming the first team in the competition's 30-year history to go the entire season undefeated.

However, that all changed in dramatic fashion on the afternoon of Saturday, 5 August 2000.

Easton entered the home match against Essex visitors Brightlingsea knowing that victory would ensure them of promotion to Division Two for the following season.

There was no sign of the sequence of events that was about to unfold as Easton, batting first, reached seven for no wicket. And then the collapse began...

Seven for no wicket soon became eight for 4, before they lost their last six wickets without scoring another run to be 14 all out!

Veteran Richard Dove, 42, was the destroyer-in-chief, returning figures of 7-2-9-6, while 20-year-old opening partner Wes Barton claimed 7-3-4-3.

Easton skipper Fred Mitchell told me: "The match will always be one of the great mysteries in the history of Easton Cricket Club. I have played for 40 years now and I have never experienced anything like that before.

"Everyone was shell-shocked – both ourselves and Brightlingsea. It was unbelievable, words can't describe it."

Brightlingsea skipper Trevor Shales was equally stunned by the chain of events.

"I think they tried to hit themselves out of trouble and played some kamikaze shots.

"It was a freak. We can beat anybody on our day, but in 30 years of playing I have never known a score like that."

Indeed, not only was Easton's undefeated run over but it was the lowest recorded score in the league history, comfortably eclipsing the 26 compiled by Harwich & Dovercourt in 1995.

The career of former Ipswich & East Suffolk and Easton cricketer Lindsay Huggins came to an end in equally dramatic fashion.

He sent down ten overs without conceding a single run while bowling for Easton Second XI against Halstead Third XI in the Two Counties Championship in May 2010.

He returned figures of 10-10-0-2 – a total of 60 balls without any runs coming off the bat – but tweaked his left knee during the final delivery and retired hurt.

Huggins, who was fast approaching his 56th birthday, had undergone a cartilage operation on the same knee 18 months previously, and after seeking medical advice decided to call it a day.

After a first-class career spanning 17 seasons, Nadeem Shahid decided to retire in November 2004.

Although born in Karachi in Pakistan, Shahid's family moved to England and he grew up in Ipswich and went on to play for both Essex and Surrey.

I had known him since the age of 14 when he joined Copdock Cricket Club along with older brother Tan.

Nadeem was a leg spinner at that age and we would queue up in the nets to see who could dismiss him and Tan, who was a medium-pace bowler, the most times.

But as his bowling failed to develop, so he blossomed as a wristy stroke-maker and he became the youngest player to represent Suffolk at Minor Counties level at the age of just 16.

He had become an outstanding schoolboy cricketer and played for England Under-19s.

He only played once more for the full Suffolk side before joining the staff at Essex full-time in 1988, making his first-team debut the following year.

After scoring 1,000 runs in a season in 1990 for the first – and as it transpired – the only time in his career, Shahid was strongly tipped for a place on that winter's England A tour.

Graham Thorpe was selected instead and when Shahid broke a finger and missed half of the following season his career never kicked on as he had expected.

He switched to Surrey in 1995 and ended up playing a total of 148 first-class matches and played alongside some of the world's greatest players at the time – Graham Gooch, Allan Border and Mark Waugh at Essex, Waqar Younis, Alec Stewart and Saqlain Mushtaq at Surrey – to name a few.

Indeed, there were occasions when he was the only member of the Surrey side to take the field who had not played international cricket.

And that was his one regret as he looked back on his career when he spoke to me by telephone from South Africa where he was coaching in Cape Town.

"All throughout my career I assumed I was going to play for England. It is only a small regret that I never did, but it is the only one I have now that I have retired," he said.

"I have been an average county cricketer, but I have enjoyed every second of it. I have played at two of the biggest clubs and won lots of trophies – County Championships, the Benson & Hedges Cup and the Sunday League.

"I would have liked to have played for England, especially as several players I grew up with went on to play for the full England side.

"But I have made a lot of great friends and had a great time and would not swap it for the world – although one thing I won't miss is fielding at short leg!"

19. Signed, sealed, delivered

DOOR knocks were part and parcel of life working on a news desk.

But only thrice can I recall being asked to do so as a sports journalist. The second time, as previously mentioned, was the day Bobby Robson was due to travel to Newcastle United to start discussions about being the club's new manager.

The third time was after George Burley was sacked as Ipswich Town manager in October 2002, when I went round to his family home in Holbrook, just outside Ipswich.

It was almost a case of going through the motions as Burley, not surprisingly, was laying low – quite possibly he was not even at the house – and no-one came to answer the door.

On both occasions I was unsuccessful in getting an 'exclusive' interview, unlike the first time that I was asked to do a door knock.

It was in November 1997 that I found myself standing on the doorstep of Jason Dozzell, who shot to instant stardom when he became the youngest player to score in the top flight of English football.

A lot had happened to Dozzell since that day in February 1984 when, aged just 16 years and 57 days and still at the town's Chantry High School, he came off the bench to score on his Ipswich Town debut in a 3–1 win at home to Coventry City.

A local lad made good, Dozzell was sold to Tottenham Hotspur for £1.9m in August 1993, but his time at White Hart Lane was dogged by injury.

He made just 99 league and cup appearances in his four seasons with Spurs, before returning to Ipswich on loan in November 1997.

Dozzell played eight times for Town, scoring once, during his loan spell, before being released by the club.

A statement issued by the club cited 'form, cost and commitment' as the reasons for not renewing his weekly contract.

The *EADT* had received a copy of a letter of complaint sent to the club after Dozzell was seen out in Ipswich on the Saturday night following the 3–0 defeat at Charlton that afternoon.

Dozzell had been withdrawn after just 32 minutes at The Valley, suffering from the after-effects of a virus, and missed the following Tuesday's home match against Stockport.

He did not train until the Thursday, before returning to the side for the home game against Sheffield United the following Sunday. He was then subsequently released by the club.

It was with some trepidation that I knocked on Dozzell's front door in a leafy area of Ipswich. Not only was the nature of my visit a thorny subject, but I had never met or even spoken to him, so why should he give me the time of day?

Dozzell, understandably, was hesitant at first about allowing me into his family home, but I need not have worried.

As soon as I mentioned that my elder brother, Richard, had taught him at Chantry High School, I was welcomed in and sat down.

Dozzell said: "This is the second time in a week I have had to defend myself, which I am really sick about."

He told me he should have been shown the letter of complaint received by the club straightaway, claiming he was not shown it until he was told he was not being offered a contract.

He said he had to come off at Charlton because he had no energy, stating he would not have started if he still had the virus, which was the week before, but before the match he had not eaten for three days.

"I got back and went for something to eat in town. I certainly was not out until three or four o'clock in the morning."

Dozzell said that when he returned to the club he went to see

Burley, who was manager at the time, on the Thursday morning and told him what had happened.

"He told me I should not have gone out on the Saturday as Ipswich is a small place. I accepted that I put myself in that position and everything was fine. I was straight back into the team for the Sheffield game on the Sunday.

"This is the last time I want to talk about it – people can draw their own conclusions," said Dozzell.

The 29-year-old said he had not got over his release by his hometown club and had not even thought about joining another club.

However, Dozzell continued to play professionally for a further five years with Northampton Town and then Colchester United, before a persistent toe injury forced him to retire, and he then managed both Ipswich Wanderers and Leiston.

Stock car commentator Jim Gregory also knew what it was like to be told his services were no longer required before he even took up the job on a regular basis.

But Gregory subsequently went on to commentate on more than 25,000 stock cars races!

He initially took up the microphone as a disc jockey through his love of music, and dabbled with commentating at Foxhall Stadium in Ipswich when regular commentator John Earrey was not available.

I interviewed Gregory, then aged 61, ahead of the annual Spede Weekend at Foxhall in 2008.

He told me: "By my own admission I was not very good and I received a letter saying that they did not think I was ever really going to make it as a commentator and to instead concentrate on being a DJ!"

But when Spedeworth, the largest stock car promoter in Europe who already ran meetings in Ipswich and Yarmouth, opened up a new track at Cleethorpes in Lincolnshire in 1982 on Sundays, Gregory was asked if he would do the commentary.

He recalled: "The meetings at Cleethorpes ran from 7pm until 10 or 11pm and I would get back home around 3am, so you can see why there were not many takers for the job!"

Gregory's commentaries improved to the extent that he found himself spending five nights a week commentating and working just two nights as a DJ, in addition to holding down a full-time job!

He had worked for Essex County Council since 1964, spending a few years as a registrar of births, deaths and marriages, before becoming finance officer.

Gregory said: "By the time I left in 1987 I was in charge of an annual budget of £52m which was not bad for someone who did not get their mathematics 'O' Level, although I subsequently passed at night school."

Within a couple of years he was commentating on around 100 meetings a year at tracks all over the country including Aldershot, Cleethorpes, Eastbourne, Rye House, Swaffham, Wimbledon and Wisbech.

He would also fill in, when required, at other tracks such as Boston, Hednesford, Mallory Park and Rockingham.

Gregory told me he had missed just one meeting in the quarter of a century he had been commentating – at Wimbledon in 1997, after accidentally poking himself in the eye.

The eye was still watering ten minutes later so he went to Clacton Hospital, which was close to where he was living at the time, to get it looked at.

"I was told I had scratched the retina. They put an eye patch on me and said I could not possibly drive home, let alone drive to Wimbledon for the meeting."

Part Five
– Off-pitch

20. Building blocks

━━━━━━━━━━━━━━━━━━━━━━━━━━

ON 17 January 1995 a crowd of 518 packed into Hadleigh United's Millfield ground to see the home team defeat Halstead United 3–2 in an FA Vase fourth-round replay.

That win set up a visit to London to face Met Police in the last 16 of the competition, where the Brettsiders lost 4–1 to end their dreams of an appearance in the Final at Wembley.

Hadleigh's success had come on the back of a host of big-name signings, including ex-Ipswich Town and Chelsea goalkeeper Jason Winters as a full-time professional.

But it had come at a crippling cost as debts amounting to several thousand pounds had built up and the club came close to folding after 103 years in existence.

It was then that Rolf Beggerow, a qualified accountant working in IT, took over as the club's treasurer – and, with the help of others, set about rebuilding the club's fortunes.

After steadying the ship Beggerow said it was around the turn of the Millennium that he set out his future vision for the club.

Phase one saw the pot-holed car park replaced by a proper 90-space car park at a cost of £33,000.

Phase two – a new changing room block for players and officials – followed at a cost of £110,000.

Phase three was carried out in four stages before being completed in 2009 and involved new toilet facilities, a visitors' lounge and refurbishing the bar and the main clubhouse at a cost of £45,000.

The club was indebted to some generous grants from the Football

Stadia Improvement Fund, a grant from the district council and a grant and loan from the town council plus the club's own fundraising scheme.

Increased levels of sponsorship also helped the club to get rid of the debt, and extra revenue generated through increased attendances and the bar meant the club could afford to employ a part-time bar steward.

The completion of the work coincided with Hadleigh, under manager Steve Jay, winning promotion to the Premier Division of the Ridgeons League after a 12-year absence.

Beggerow told me: "It is the realisation of a vision and I take a lot of satisfaction from seeing it all come together. A lot of hard work and many hours have gone into improving the ground."

The club have continued to go from strength-to-strength and reached the quarter-finals of the FA Vase in the 2012–13 season, before losing to Tunbridge Wells.

No-one deserved to enjoy the moment more than Beggerow, who by then was chairman, when the club won the Thurlow Nunn League Premier Division title for the first time in their history on the final day of the 2013–14 season.

Needham Market, like Hadleigh United, used to play in the Suffolk & Ipswich League. In fact, only 30 years ago they were playing in Division Eight – a whopping 11 divisions lower than Division One North of the Ryman League.

But in March 2011 they were on the verge of promotion to the Ryman Premier Division, involved in an exciting two-horse race with East Thurrock United at the top of the table.

It was another story of a remarkable rise of a non-league club, albeit under different circumstances, to that of Hadleigh United.

Danny Laws was appointed manager after Mark Morsley, who had guided Needham to promotion from Division One of the Ridgeons League in 2004–05, took over at higher-league AFC Sudbury.

Playing for Needham at the time were two ex-professionals – goalkeeper Danny Gay, who had played for Southend, and Kevin Horlock, who won 32 caps for Northern Ireland and appeared in the Premier League for both Swindon Town and Manchester City.

He then spent two years with Ipswich Town, before injuries brought an end to his professional career after 17 seasons.

Horlock, who joined Needham at the start of the 2008–09 season, said: "I didn't want to play for the sake of playing – I wanted to be a part of something and I have been proved right in every sense.

"I have absolutely loved it," added the then 38-year-old.

So much so that although Needham missed out on promotion that season, when the club started up their own Academy, Horlock stayed on to run it and has since turned down offers from professional clubs.

The club finally won promotion to the Premier Division of the Ryman League as champions of Division One North at the end of the 2014–15 season.

From small acorns do large trees grow…

Mildenhall Cricket Club chairman Mike Clarke and fellow club stalwarts could be forgiven for feeling misty-eyed when Suffolk faced Nottinghamshire in June 2001.

The club's Wamil Way ground had been chosen to stage the Cheltenham & Gloucester Trophy third-round tie against Notts, whose side included a relatively unknown all-rounder called Kevin Pietersen.

It was the realisation of a dream for Clarke to host a first-class county at Mildenhall's idyllic headquarters, the club's home since 1972.

The dream started in the early 1960s when a group of members set about raising money to fund a new ground.

Clarke, together with Mike Kill and Tony Cornell, realised that if the club were to progress they needed to move from Recreation Way, which they shared with the football club.

They decided to raise money through bingo.

Clarke recalled: "We offered cash prizes before Rank and Mecca started to do so and it soon became so popular that we had to move to a bigger venue.

"We switched to the Town Hall and we were packing it out. Everyone was talking about it and we were doing really well.

"It was then that we were closed down by the police because what we were doing was deemed illegal."

However, about a year later there was a test case in the House of Lord's which was won and so the bingo sessions started up again.

By 1968–69 a site was chosen and the club had agreed to buy the land.

Around £6,000 had been made through bingo – a figure put into perspective by the fact that in the mid-1960s you could buy a house for around £2,500–£3,000!

The club had provisionally been promised grant money for two-thirds of the cost if they could find a third towards their target of £18,000.

Although the 11-acre site only cost £3,000, clearing and levelling plus laying the grass cost £5,000–£6,000 and the pavilion a further £8,000 to build, bringing the total to around £18,000.

Clarke remembered: "We were ready to play the first game in June 1972. I faced the first-ever ball to be bowled and square cut it for four – and it was a cracking shot!"

Another man whose vision became a success story that I featured was Brian Potter, who was chairman of the Potters Leisure Resort.

Potters, which is based in the tiny village of Hopton-on-Sea on the Norfolk/Suffolk border, is to indoor bowls what Wembley is to football and Lord's is to cricket.

The resort dates back to 1920 when Herbert Potter set up the first-ever permanent structure holiday camp thanks to winning £500 in a national newspaper competition.

Herbert was the grandfather of Brian Potter, who took over the business with wife Judy in 1984 when his father passed away.

Although Potters employed 250 staff in the 18-week holiday season between May and September, and started running occasional weekend breaks, Brian was having to stand staff off between Monday and Friday.

During a visit to the resort in January 2009, Potter told me over lunch: "I had to think of something which would allow the business to develop and grow.

"I wanted to create a 52-week a year business, and the challenge was to think of something to extend the season on the cold, draughty east coast.

"It was while shaving one day that I thought 'what do retired people do?' Bowls was undergoing a quiet revolution and I could see a market for retired people."

The Potters decided to build two indoor rinks to test the water, but demand outstripped supply and so it was decided to build a further six the following year.

He approached the World Bowls Council with his plan that he would be prepared to build a 'plug and play' stadium if they would move from Preston, home to the World Indoor Championships since 1986.

Despite their lack of interest he decided to gamble and build a £2.5 million, six-rink stadium – and managed to attract the English Ladies' Championships instead.

"Word soon got around the bowls circuit that Potters was the place where you could be catered for and entertained all on one site, as opposed to at Preston where people stayed in hotels or guest houses and had to get to the Guild Hall," he recalled.

Organisers of the World Indoor Championships decided to move from Preston to Potters the following year – and the rest, as they say, is history.

Potters is now world renowned and stages events throughout the year, although sadly Brian Potter is no longer with us after passing away, aged 73, in November 2014.

21. Fan-tastic supporters

THE chairman of Norwich United was surely having a laugh.

He had just told me that the woman sitting in front of me in the stand at Felixstowe & Walton United's ground was not Andrew 'Porky' Claydon's mum but his No.1 fan!

But I was still convinced John Hilditch was winding me up.

I had got to know Hilditch, a successful self-made businessman, while my son Ben was playing for Norwich United in the first half of the 2008–09 season.

But I did not know him well enough to be sure he was not pulling the wool over my eyes until he started to engage in a conversation with her to prove otherwise.

I could still scarcely believe it, and was so intrigued that I immediately introduced myself to her and asked if I could interview her for my weekly 'Scene & Heard' column in the *Evening Star*.

Her name was Jean Osborne and she lived in a tiny village between Sudbury and Bury St Edmunds.

The 68-year-old said she had first watched Claydon when he joined AFC Sudbury at the start of the 2000–01 season.

She told me: "I used to go to watch Sudbury before he played there, and then he came along and that was it.

"He became my favourite and when he was at Sudbury he presented me with a lovely signed photograph of himself."

After Claydon left the club in the summer of 2007, so Jean switched her allegiance too.

Claydon played at Mildenhall Town and Felixstowe & Walton,

before signing for Norwich United, and Jean, together with 74-year-old partner Dennis Watts, had continued to follow him around.

The then 33-year-old striker said: "I am very honoured as not many people at our level of football get this. I have grown to know Jean because she has followed my career closely for so many years.

"I have had children of my own and even taken my little boy to see her because Jean wanted to meet him. She is a really nice lady."

Even Jean could not claim to have travelled as far and wide as Gerald Blagdurn, who could claim to be Suffolk's No.1 cricket fan.

Gerald started to follow the fortunes of the Minor Counties side when Derek Randall joined Suffolk in 1994.

And even though Randall retired after a seven-year stint with the county, Gerald continued to travel from his home just outside Nottingham to see Suffolk play.

He was still regularly seen supporting Suffolk at matches more than a decade after Randall had played his last game!

It was in the summer of 2010 that I sat with Gerald and chatted to him about his devotion to following Suffolk's fortunes.

He explained that Randall was his favourite cricketer during his Nottinghamshire days, so after the ex-England batsman signed for Suffolk, Gerald decided to follow him.

However, he got off to an inauspicious start when Randall made his debut against Cumberland at Kendal in 1994.

"There are three cricket grounds in Kendal, and I went to all three before I arrived at the right one! By the time I got there I had missed Derek bat in the first innings!" Gerald recalled.

Gerald had already ensured there would be no such dramas in finding Suffolk's home grounds, visiting each one of them before the season started so he knew where to go.

The 62-year-old civil servant, who used his holiday to attend Suffolk's fixtures, said he used to book into guest houses close to where Suffolk were playing.

"I then found this place – The Bull at Woolpit – and I have stayed there ever since for home matches and travel from there each day.

"I usually book up in February and normally stay overnight on Saturday, Sunday and Monday for a three-day fixture."

It was around that time that Randall retired from Minor Counties cricket, and Gerald admitted: "I thought I would not watch Suffolk once Derek stopped playing.

"However, I had taken out a life membership and I liked the people who play for the county and the friendly atmosphere, so I have continued to support them."

Two fan-tastic supporters I reported on in the *EADT* were identical twins who became promotion rivals – at the ripe old age of 79!

Jim and Henry Hammond were avid supporters of Hadleigh United and FC Clacton respectively.

And in the 2008–09 season the two clubs were both battling for promotion from Division One of the Ridgeons League.

After spotting the two brothers together when FC Clacton hosted Hadleigh United, I got chatting to them and arranged to interview them about their friendly rivalry at the return fixture a few weeks later.

It was Jim who was celebrating come the end of the season, Hadleigh finishing runners-up behind Newmarket Town and winning promotion, while Henry and FC Clacton missed out and the Essex club had to wait another season before reaching the top flight.

Football fans travelling the length and breadth of the country is part and parcel of the modern-day game, but more than half-a-century ago it was not as common as there were far less cars on the road.

My father, Cyril, was among 3,000 Ipswich Town supporters who made the long trek to Old Trafford to see their team face the mighty Manchester United in an FA Cup fourth-round tie in 1958.

The match was the last to be played at the ground by the 'Busby Babes' before the Munich air disaster just 12 days later – and he recalled his adventure as part of my feature on the 50th anniversary of the crash.

A lifelong Town fan, who had followed the club's fortunes since 1934, he said it was hard for football fans today to appreciate the magnitude of the occasion.

My dad, who travelled by train with his parents and two brothers, Peter and Arthur, explained that those supporters who made the trek north were watching United play for the first time.

He said: "United's young side had developed into arguably the best team in the country, while Town were at that stage comparatively unknown – they had just gained promotion from Division Three (South) and were standing in mid-table in Division Two.

"In the early 1950s, far from every household had a television set and football generally was not publicised in the way it is today.

"The visit to Manchester United, therefore, was a completely new experience – an adventure which few of Town's supporters would have undertaken previously."

As for the tie itself, which United won 2–0, he recalled: "At the end of the game, United knew they had been severely tested by their less illustrious opponents and the home crowd were quick to appreciate and acknowledge the Town's performance and gave them a standing ovation as they left the pitch."

Fant-tastic.

22. Breaking the law

ONCE is a mistake, twice a coincidence, three times a pattern, so the saying goes.

It was an embarrassing pattern so far as Woodbridge Town were concerned in the 2009–10 football season, when the club fielded three ineligible players – two of them in the same game!

The Woodpeckers first came under investigation in November of that season, after Ben Miller came on as a substitute in an FA Vase second round proper tie at Ely City, which ended in a 1–1 draw.

I got wind of the alleged offence and ran a story saying the scheduled replay the following Wednesday was postponed while the Football Association carried out an investigation.

The club were subsequently thrown out of the competition after they were found guilty of playing Miller while he was suspended after picking up five bookings.

Miller later told me: "I missed the midweek game before the tie with flu, but said I would go and sit on the bench in an emergency.

"We were 1–0 up when I came on with ten minutes to go and they equalised, so the match went to extra-time and I struggled through that."

It was a costly mistake, the club losing out on much-needed potential revenue from the replay, and the £1,200 prize money they would have pocketed had they won.

If that was not bad enough, Woodbridge slipped up again the following January.

Their joy at winning 5–1 at Felixstowe & Walton United in the

Thurlow Nunn League Premier Division – a match I covered – soon turned to despair.

Under the *Evening Star's* back page heading 'Woe-bridge as probe launched' I reported that the cub were again under investigation after two players – Ben Seaman and substitute Glenn Snell – allegedly played whilst suspended.

Woodbridge were found guilty of the offence and the match was ordered to be replayed. To add insult to injury, Felixstowe won the replayed fixture 5–0!

The Kingsley Healthcare Suffolk & Ipswich League Representative side were booted out of the FA Inter League Cup in November 2011 – not for playing a suspended player but one who was too young!

Elliot Crowe of Ransomes Sports was the player in question as he did not celebrate his 16th birthday until the previous August and players had to be 16 on 1 January of that year.

The story also made the back page of the *Evening Star* after SIL chairman Keith Norton came into our office and admitted to me that he had made an oversight.

Norton said he took full responsibility for the error and even went so far as to offer his resignation to the league's committee, although this had been rejected.

It was certainly tough on the SIL side, who had beaten the Reading League 3–0 the previous month to reach the last 16 of the competition. They were expelled and the Reading League reinstated in their place.

Two stories I wrote in the space of six months in 2012 were as a result of matches that ended in a furore – and my youngest son, Ben, was involved in both.

The first was while he was playing for Felixstowe & Walton United, who were hit with eight charges arising out of their Thurlow Nunn League Premier Division match at home to Hadleigh United in March of that year.

Ben was sent off (harshly, I might add, which led to much of the animosity that followed) and his Felixstowe team-mate Josh Capocci also received his matching orders during the match from Colchester-based referee John Magill.

Seven of the charges had been brought by Suffolk FA and related to the two players and the management team using improper conduct/bringing the game into disrepute and using insulting words or behaviour.

The eighth charge, brought by the Ridgeons League, related to having more than the requisite number of officials standing up in the technical area.

Club chairman Andy Wilding was quick to defend the Seasiders' reputation in the wake of what he described as 'just a bad day at the office' after Hadleigh won the fiercely-contested derby 2–1.

That was nothing compared to the match that saw Ipswich Sunday Morning League side Maidenhall have FOUR players sent off and SIX booked (Ben was not among them) in a league match at Wickham Market the following October.

Official Ollie Morris-Sanders, not surprisingly, abandoned the match mid-way through the second period with the sides – Wickham Market also had a player dismissed – drawing 3–3.

On another occasion a team-mate of Ben's who was sent off paid the ultimate price by subsequently being banned for a national Cup Final.

The player in question was Nick Middlebrook, who by his own admission was left 'bitterly disappointed' after learning he was to miss out on playing for Suffolk FA in their FA County Youth Cup Final against Cambridgeshire FA.

Middlebrook was dismissed for using foul and abusive language just ten minutes after coming on as a substitute for Suffolk Under-18s in their 5–2 victory over Hertfordshire FA in an East Anglian Counties Championship match in March 2008.

The 18-year-old striker, who vented his frustration at the referee after he felt he was fouled, was hit with a two-match ban that took in the Final at Portman Road.

Suffolk manager Andy Gould said: "I have known him since he was 14 and what he said was completely out of character for someone who comes from a lovely family."

Gould, who was a great man-manager in my opinion, ensured that Middlebrook was unofficially involved on the day and he was even included on the team photograph with the trophy after the match which Suffolk won 2–1.

The reputation of some players precedes them on the football pitch, and two of the most consistent offenders locally in recent years have been Neil Calver and Danny Cunningham.

Both are talented footballers, but have regularly had brushes with authority and I was keen to interview them to find out more about the personalities behind the players.

When I interviewed Calver while he was at Leiston in January 2012, he admitted he had been booked more times than he cared to remember during his career.

The softly-spoken Calver, who played for AFC Sudbury, Felixstowe Port & Town and again when they later became Felixstowe & Walton United, Hadleigh United, Leiston, Woodbridge Town and Whitton United, told me: "There was a spell one season where I got targeted by referees.

"Once you get a reputation you are going to, but I think I have never been a malicious or dirty player, but I do go in hard because if you don't you get hurt yourself.

"My worst season was when I was at AFC Sudbury and I was summoned to Soho Square to see the FA. I had received 20 yellow cards at the time, and ended the season with 24 – which was about one every three games – as I played the majority of games that season."

Calver holds the unusual distinction of both scoring and being sent off in FA Vase Finals while playing for AFC Sudbury.

He was dismissed after coming on as a substitute against Winchester City at St Andrew's in 2004.

"I came on when we were losing 1–0. I tried to make what I thought was the right decision at the time," he said of being shown a red card for committing a professional foul and conceding a penalty to prevent an almost certain goal.

However, Winchester scored from the spot to condemn AFC Sudbury to a 2–0 defeat – just 12 months after they lost 2–1 to Brigg Town at Upton Park.

Calver scored from the penalty spot in injury time in the 2005 FA Vase Final against Didcot Town at White Hart Lane, but it was too little, too late as AFC Sudbury this time lost 3–2 to complete an unwanted hat-trick of final losses.

Few players polarised opinion as much as Danny Cunningham, the mercurial and enigmatic left winger who has played for all five of Suffolk's top clubs – AFC Sudbury, Bury Town, Leiston, Lowestoft and Needham Market – during his chequered career.

Cunningham was jailed for possessing drugs with intent to supply, after being arrested as the Leiston team coach arrived for an FA Cup fourth qualifying round replay at Lewes in November 2008.

I had covered the first match, a 1–1 draw at Leiston's Victory Road ground when Cunningham scored with a cross that went in off the far post.

David Rees, the club's press officer, agreed to cover the replay down in Sussex for us and I requested that he sent us the teams on the bottom of the report.

However, he didn't include the line-ups and when I spoke to him the following day I asked him if Cunningham had played as he was not mentioned in the report. He admitted he hadn't, but was reluctant to tell me why and referred me to Andy Crisp, the club's chairman.

Crisp told me of Cunningham's arrest at which point I passed the story on to the *EADT* news desk. Cunningham pleaded guilty to the charge and served nine months of a two-year sentence in Norwich Prison.

Four years on I interviewed Cunningham, by then playing for Lowestoft Town, who had been described as being like 'Marmite' by boss Richard Wilkins, who had twice signed him for Bury Town.

Cunningham said: "I can see why people say that, but people that know me see me differently. I am a different person off the pitch to on it. I have had my disciplinary problems but that is how I play."

23. Double acts

_____

ONE played up front, the other led from the front.

One was Scottish, the other English.

One played football, the other cricket.

However, both became adopted sons of East Anglia and international sportsmen who saw their careers ended prematurely by injury, before joining forces to co-host a breakfast radio sports show.

Ex-Scotland international striker Alan Brazil, and Ronnie Irani, the former Essex cricket captain and England all-rounder, had never met before fate threw them together on talkSPORT radio.

Although both were well-known to me and I had interviewed them before, the opportunity to interview the pair of them together was too tempting to resist.

After presenting their show from the County Ground at Chelmsford prior to the club's annual Press Day in 2011, we sat down together, surrounded by piles of chairs in the executive box used by the Essex committee on match days.

Brazil, a colourful and sometimes controversial character – he had been sacked by talkSPORT in 2004 but was reinstated after complaints from listeners – retired from football due to a back injury at the age of 27.

An offer to co-commentate on Ipswich Town matches handed him his initial break in broadcasting and 'eased' him back into football after he had fallen out of love with the game when his career was cut short.

That led to work with BBC Radio Five Live and then working for

Sky TV covering the Nationwide League, but after five years he got frustrated as he wasn't getting any Premier League games and decided it was time to move on.

Brazil said: "I went to talkSPORT and that was just a bit of fun, to be honest, in the evenings when there was probably 50 cab drivers listening, but amazingly it progressed from doing that to doing the breakfast show, which was more serious, and 11 years later I am still here."

Although Irani had done a drive time show for Chelmsford radio station Dream 107 on Friday evenings in the winter, when his knees finally succumbed to the pain and medical advice at the age of 35, he did not know what the future held.

He said: "I kind of fell into the job really. I had just retired and three or four days later I got a phone call from talkSPORT saying they were thinking about having a change and did I fancy getting involved in the breakfast show with Alan Brazil and what did I think?

"I said 'yes' without even thinking about it and then realised I would have to get up at four o'clock in the morning, but I love every minute of it."

The pair had been a double act for close on four years and it was easy to see how they fed off each other and the 'buzz' they got from doing the show together.

They continued to present the show for a further two years, before Irani suddenly departed in May 2013.

A pair of twins were creating a buzz of their own in the Ridgeons League at Premier Division side Stanway Rovers.

Ben and Sam Newson were not identical twins, but the brothers were causing double trouble for defences.

I met the twins at their family home in East Bergholt in February 2010 one evening before they went off to training.

The 21-year-olds had played for the same senior clubs, did the same job and even drove the same cars, but told me they craved to be treated as individuals.

It was clear they had a mischievous streak and they admitted they had tried to use this to their advantage in the past.

Ben said: "I will admit I have occasionally tried to confuse the referee when he has warned me a few times and I am obviously going to be booked the next time.

"If I then make a rash challenge and the referee comes over I have said 'It wasn't me – it's him you've been speaking to' and sometimes the referees do think about it and wonder, but to be fair to the referees most of the time they do get it right!"

Sam added: "It is good to have a bit of banter with the referee. They know that we are twins and that we are going to push it, so why not have a bit of fun with it?"

He also recalled: "When we were younger we were identical, but the older we have got the more ugly we have become! But when you see us on the pitch we are so alike it is unbelievable. You get defenders saying 'Oh s**t, there's two of you' so that can be quite amusing."

Martin Head and Don James, who were joint managers of Sudbury Town, were a successful double act.

The pair had led Sudbury to the FA Vase Final at Wembley in 1989 and in doing so became the first Suffolk side – indeed the first from the Eastern Counties League – to reach the Final.

They had come agonisingly close the previous season, losing 2–0 in the second leg of the semi-final at Colne Dynamoes to go out 3–1 on aggregate.

Speaking ahead of the club staging a 20th anniversary reunion of reaching the Final, James said: "I took the view that if we got that near again to Wembley we would be very lucky. I just could not see it happening two years in a row."

In fact, so disappointed was club chairman Ron Ashdown and his fellow directors Danny Crosbie and Terry Drake at Sudbury's semi-final exit, it was not until after the last game of the season that they told Head and James they were to be kept on!

Not only had the club reached the semi-finals of the Vase, Sudbury finished third in the Eastern Counties League, lost in the League Cup semi-final and lifted the Suffolk FA Premier Cup in what was the pair's first season in charge.

But it was success in the Vase that the club craved at the time.

So, the following season, when they reached the last four of the competition again, Sudbury were determined to not let the opportunity pass them by a second time.

However, they were fortunate to escape from the first leg away to Hungerford Town with a goalless draw thanks to an outstanding display by goalkeeper Dean Garnham.

Head recalled: "We travelled up on the Friday night and stayed in a lovely hotel. In fact, it was so good that the players probably over-indulged in using the saunas and swimming pool!"

Sudbury made no mistake in the second leg the following Saturday as a crowd of 4,320 crammed into The Priory (I left our family holiday base near Scarborough early that morning and drove back) to see the Suffolk side thrash their opponents 6–0.

They were boosted by two goals in the opening six minutes, the first from full back Marty Thorpe, who was persuaded to play by his wife Denise just hours after the couple lost the twins they were expecting two months later.

Thorpe missed the pre-match lunch and arrived late, but just two minutes and 12 seconds after kick-off he netted the crucial first goal from a free-kick and set his side on course for Wembley.

Head and James recalled one of the biggest talking points ahead of the Final, surrounded who would lead the team out.

Football Association policy dictated that only one manager was allowed the honour, but Sudbury requested that both Head and James should be allowed to do so.

Although Head offered to stand down if there was not a change of policy, a compromise was reached following a last-minute complaint by their opponents Tamworth and James led the team out with Head at the rear of the line.

The match ended as a 1–1 draw after extra time, meaning a replay at Peterborough United's London Road ground the following Wednesday.

Head recalled: "It all felt rather strange. All the players went up to the Royal Box and shook hands with Pat Jennings, the chief guest, but there was nothing to celebrate or commiserate over."

The attendance of 27,552 produced gate receipts of £120,000, with Sudbury and Tamworth picking up £17,000 apiece – a tidy sum back then.

The sense of anti-climax was even greater for Sudbury four days later, Tamworth winning the replay 3–0 in front of 11,200 fans.

James recalled: "Twenty years down the line I still sit and think about what we achieved.

"That Sudbury side was one of the best local sides I have ever seen, even if it was my team.

"When we played in the competition, the bottom half of the leagues above were allowed to enter. The Ridgeons League clubs when they play in the FA Vase now are like the Premier League clubs are in the FA Cup."

Not only did Sudbury reach the Vase Final that season, the club won the Eastern Counties League, the League Cup and also the Premier Cup!

And just for good measure they also reached the fourth qualifying round of the FA Cup, before losing 1–0 at home in a replay to Aylesbury, meaning they were included in the draw for the first round proper.

24. Saturday Night Fever

IT was the only time that I ever used just one word in more than 25 years of writing headlines.

As each goal flew in so I re-wrote the headline and as the words got fewer, so the type face got bigger and bigger.

By the time the eighth goal hit the net I was left with one word that stretched across the whole of the front page: it quite simply said 'HUMILIATED!'

There was no other way to describe the events of 4 March 1995 on the front page of the *Green 'Un*, the Saturday night football paper published in Ipswich.

Manchester United went on to crush Ipswich Town 9–0 at Old Trafford – still the biggest win in Premier League history.

It gave me absolutely no pleasure to write such a headline, but it remains one of the stand-out memories of my three years as editor of the *Green 'Un*.

Launched in 1923, the *Green 'Un* served Suffolk and North East Essex as a printed newspaper until it re-launched as a website at the start of the 2008–09 season.

The *Green 'Un* branding lives on in print form through the name given to the sports pages of both the *EADT* and *Evening Star*.

I have lost count of the number of times I have been asked over the years why it was decided to pull the plug on printing the *Green 'Un*.

The simple reason that time was called on the much-loved paper was that sales had declined beyond the point where publishers Archant Ltd could no longer justify it.

The *Green 'Un* had been making a small loss for a number of years, but had continued to print because of the backlash that would accompany the loss of such a much-loved publication.

In its heyday sales were around 20,000 per week, but that was when there were not even any local radio stations to provide competitive opposition.

Apart from goal updates on *Grandstand* and *World of Sport* – the respective Saturday afternoon programmes on BBC1 and ITV – there was no other way of following Ipswich Town's progress on a Saturday afternoon.

But it was not just the coverage of Ipswich Town and Colchester United that led to soaring sales – non-league football was covered with weekly club notes and there were also reports from around 30 local matches.

These reports were phoned through at half-time and again at full-time to half-a-dozen or so copytakers, before being passed to the sub-editors, who then checked them for accuracy before sending them off to go on the page.

Due to the speed that the paper was produced – matches kicking-off at 3pm didn't end until around 4.40pm in those days and the *Green 'Un* was on sale soon after 6pm – it was not uncommon for mistakes to creep through.

My favourite that appeared in print was when someone passed to a team-mate who 'shit against the post' – a case of foul play if ever there was one...

Such mistakes were part and parcel of the *Green 'Un*, and in some way even added to its appeal.

Saturday Night Fever would be repeated across Suffolk and north-east Essex as large queues would form (200–300 would congregate weekly on the Cornhill in both Ipswich and Bury St Edmunds) awaiting the bundles of papers hot off the press.

In my early teenage years my Saturday night would revolve

around reading that day's *Evening Star*, followed by the *Green 'Un* and then watching *Match of the Day*.

Maybe it was my destiny to one day be editor of the *Green 'Un*, and in the summer of 1993 I was proud to be appointed to the role to enable Tony Garnett to concentrate on editing the sports pages of the *EADT* and *Evening Star*.

The *Green 'Un* had by then returned to being a football-only newspaper, after a period when other sports had been introduced in a bid to drive sales up.

It was under my stewardship that the *Green 'Un* celebrated the publication of its 2,500th edition on Saturday, 16 December 1995, although no-one could be sure that the landmark was indeed reached on that day!

Each week the edition number on the front page was supposed to be updated, but I knew that on occasions this had not been the case, so it is anyone's guess when the 2,500th edition was really published.

In an attempt to try to halt sliding sales I introduced new ideas and columns, one of which was instrumental in launching the media career of ex-Ipswich Town striker Alan Brazil, who also played for Tottenham Hotspur, Manchester United, Coventry City and Queens Park Rangers.

My colleague Mel Henderson, who used to be the public relations officer at Ipswich Town, had heard Brazil on BBC Radio Suffolk's Friday night round table programme, where local sports celebrities would chew the fat on the week's sporting events.

He thought Brazil's forthright and sometimes outspoken views would transfer into a lively column in print, and so I arranged to meet with him after a match at Portman Road at the back of the stand where the Press Box was situated.

I had been told that I was not allowed to exceed a budget of £70 a week, so I pulled off a coup when the former Scottish international agreed to sign for the *Green 'Un* for £50 per week!

Henderson wrote 'Pele's Viewpoint' after speaking to Brazil each week and it became such a popular column that within a few months Brazil's column was 'transferred' across to the *Evening Star* and he doubled his weekly salary!

The wider platform to air his views saw Brazil get bigger and better offers of media work and led to him working for Sky TV, before joining TalkSPORT and hosting his own breakfast show.

During my time in the editor's chair – I was in charge of the paper until I became sports editor of the *EADT* in October 2006 – sales were around 7,000–8,000 per week.

Sales figures had fallen steadily over the years, the arrival of Radio Orwell in October 1975 the first to have an impact, before BBC Radio Suffolk took to the airwaves in April 1990 to further reduce the need to purchase the paper.

The increasing number of Saturday afternoons without an Ipswich Town fixture – Premier League matches being scheduled for screening on Sky TV on a Sunday or Monday plus blank Saturdays due to the introduction of international weekends – saw sales suffer further during my spell as editor and thereafter.

With fewer people buying the paper, newsagents were no longer prepared to stay open late on a Saturday evening to sell it, and supermarkets and garages became the main outlets.

The arrival of the Internet was the final nail in the coffin of the *Green 'Un*. With information now available online the decision was made to print the Saturday night paper for the last time, and instead re-launch it as a website.

Part Six
– Highs and lows

25. Fighting for their lives

───────────────

IT was just as well that Lee Wilcox was sat across the other side of the room.

If he had been sat closer he would surely have seen the tears that were welling up in my eyes as he described the horrific last few months of his young life.

Lee, a talented footballer who was playing for Brantham Athletic in Division One of the Ridgeons League at the time, had been diagnosed with testicular cancer at the age of just 17.

After initially being told he had an 80 percent chance of survival, Lee's parents were subsequently delivered the spine-chilling news that the prognosis was actually worse than they had been led to believe.

His parents, Lee senior and Rachel, had not told him that doctors feared he had only a 50-50 chance of survival as he underwent 10 weeks of energy-sapping chemotherapy for testicular cancer.

Lee senior recalled: "He had steroids with the first chemo treatment, but he reacted to the steroids and the side effects left him depressed, suffering from anxiety and unable to sleep.

"He also had an ulcerated mouth, right down to the back of his throat."

However, Lee's strength and fitness, coupled with his determination to beat the disease, which had spread to his liver, lungs and lymph glands, was to stand him in good stead.

Lee spent Christmas in hospital and was so ill he didn't want to open his presents, but said his 18th birthday on 17 January was worse, even though he was allowed home for the weekend.

However, just ten weeks after entering St Bartholomew's Hospital in London on 10 December 2009, Lee displayed his fighting spirit by refusing the aid of a wheelchair and walked out with his dad supporting him instead.

He was determined to return to action as soon as possible, and slowly but surely started to build up his fitness.

Just a month after returning to the family home in Ipswich, Lee amazed doctors by playing again.

He made an emotional return to action when he appeared as a substitute for Brantham's Under-18 team, managed by his father, on the night that they won the Southern Division title of the Ridgeons Youth League at Hadleigh United's Millfield ground.

Lee senior recalled: "It was 2–1 with 20 minutes to go, but I said to coach Paul Skingley, who runs the team with me, I am not putting him on at 2–1, but luckily we went 3–1 up then 4–1 and so I said 'let's get him on' and he got a standing ovation.

"I looked round and some of the Brantham mums were wiping the tears away from their faces and that was hard. To see them and knowing what Lee had been through brought it home to me.

"I could feel everyone's eyes looking at me and I was wiping the tears away. I just looked round and saw one of the Brantham mums looking at me so I looked away but then looked back and she was crying her eyes out as well. I was just very emotional, but it was a great night."

Listening to Lee tell me his story was a real roller-coaster of emotions as he went into detail – some of which the *EADT* did not print as it was either so gruesome or the sub-editor did not believe what I had actually written to be correct – before the uplifting ending.

And it had certainly been worth the wait – I had known of Lee's illness before Christmas as Lee senior used to run the Bourne Vale Hawks football team along with my elder brother Richard and they still kept in touch.

Via Richard I had asked if I could do an article on Lee's battle with cancer, but at the family's request I had to remain patient for three months.

Only after Lee was back playing again were they willing to allow me into their home to interview Lee and his dad.

Lee is still playing football locally, and only an injury sustained just before the semi-final prevented him from appearing for Touchline SIL side Ipswich Valley Rangers in the Suffolk FA Senior Cup Final in May 2015.

It was a similar scenario so far as Suffolk cricketer Russell Catley was concerned.

I had known Russell for around 15 years and even went on the same cricket tour to Australia with him while he was a pupil at Ipswich School.

His world was turned upside down when he was diagnosed with a brain tumour after suffering a fit in his sleep in July 2004.

Following a brain scan in mid-August he was told there was an abnormality.

Russell recalled: "I was absolutely devastated, but I still played in a match for Exning against Sudbury that afternoon.

"I didn't know what to do with myself, so playing cricket took my mind off it more than anything."

Initially he didn't want to tell anyone, preferring to fight it and then tell everyone once he had hopefully made a full recovery.

But as people started to find out, so Russell made the decision to tell them the truth, although he was understandably reluctant for me to write a story.

It was only on the eve of his first match the following April that my patience was rewarded and Russell spoke publicly for the first time.

He told me that because of the type of tumour it was decided it could not be surgically removed, so he had undergone a course of radiotherapy, starting in early November.

The 31-year-old, who lived in Ely, had visited Addenbrooke's Hospital in Cambridge every day for treatment for six weeks until just before Christmas.

The only side effects were losing about one-third of his hair – he decided to shave the rest off – and tiredness, resulting in him even spending three or four hours in bed on Christmas Day.

Russell, who worked for chartered surveyors Bidwells in Cambridge, said the tiredness lasted for four to six weeks throughout January, but he was able to go back to work on 11 February 2005 for three afternoons a week.

He had then returned to work full-time, apart from the odd morning when he was still feeling tired, after spending six or seven months off work on full pay.

After being encouraged to be as active as possible without tiring himself out, Russell started to visit the gym and go on brisk walks, before taking the first steps towards playing cricket again at the end of February.

He recalled: "It was really strange, but it felt good to hold a bat in my hands again. I was worried about whether my feet would be moving, and if they didn't whether it would be linked to my condition.

"But your movement at your first net session tends not to be as it should, regardless of whether you have got a brain tumour or not."

Russell, who made his debut for Suffolk in 1992 and had been a regular in the side for eight years, said he was not setting himself any targets as he had in previous seasons as he prepared to make his comeback.

That was the weekend that the article appeared in the *EADT* in April 2005, Russell scoring 25 and returning figures of 10-3-34-4 for Exning in a friendly against Mildenhall at Chippenham that afternoon.

"It is probably a cliché, but I have got a different perspective on life, and it is more important to just enjoy life and not worry about such things," he explained.

"I was reading in the paper recently a story about a guy in his mid-30s with four children from Burwell who had died from a brain tumour. A year ago I would have probably flicked past it, but I just sat there and wept.

"Colleagues say that I have got a glow about me when I come into work, which is a pretty amazing feeling for someone who has gone through what I have gone through."

26. Fears and tears

THE EMOTION came flooding out as Jo Ellis opened her heart to me.

It was in March 2009 that Ellis revealed to me during a telephone interview the extent of the illness that was threatening her career.

I had interviewed Ellis twice before, the first time in February 2006 before she left for Australia with the England Hockey squad to compete in the Commonwealth Games the following month in Melbourne.

We had met again two years later when her hopes of competing for Great Britain in the Beijing Olympics were in the balance.

The 26-year-old had spent two days in an Australian hospital after being injured in a warm-up match in Perth, and had to have air drained from a lung.

A reckless challenge by an opponent left her struggling to breathe and she was taken to hospital where X-rays revealed a pocket of air around her lung.

She also suffered what is known as a 'stinger' which had left her with neuro and soft tissue damage to her shoulder.

The injury meant she was unable to play any part in the subsequent five-match series against Australia.

It also cast a dark shadow over whether the 27-year-old Cambridge-born forward would make the cut when the 16-strong squad was announced in June.

Ellis did make the cut, but her dream of playing in the Olympics turned into a 'nightmare' and left her suffering from chronic fatigue and feeling so low she didn't want to play hockey again.

After taking part in the Olympics in September 2008 it was up to the players to decide when they returned to playing in the England Hockey League for their club sides.

Ellis planned to enjoy a welcome break and return after Christmas, but as each week went by and her name was absent from the Ipswich Ladies' team sheet, I sensed all was not well.

I spoke to Emma Millar, the club's press officer and vice chair, to get a clearer picture of the situation before approaching Ellis.

It was to turn into the most illuminating phone call I can ever recall making during my entire career as a sports journalist.

I have no doubt that she would not have been so candid had it not been for our previous interviews, but even I was taken aback as she poured her heart out over the phone.

An emotional Ellis admitted: "I was struggling throughout the Olympics. It was the toughest thing I have ever done both physically and mentally.

"There were times when I questioned things but my desire to compete at the Olympics was such that I just carried on playing."

Great Britain finished sixth in Beijing, but Ellis said: "It was a nightmare because I was not on top form. I decided that when I got back I was going to sort myself out, but it has taken much longer than I thought it would."

Ellis, who had joined Ipswich at the age of 14 and commuted from her Cambridgeshire home to training and matches every week, added: "I didn't realise until now how much I have lived on the edge over the years.

"I have always given 110 per cent in every training session because I want to be the best I can possibly be.

"I want to be 100 per cent right before I come back and start playing because I don't ever want to feel like that again.

"I was at a point where I was pretty low and didn't want to play hockey again."

Jo did briefly return to play for Ipswich, but the illness effectively ended her career as a top-class player.

Ipswich Town goalkeeper Laurie Sivell was clearly hurting and feeling much the same way after what was to prove his final game for the club in February 1984.

Sivell, who was one of several Ipswich team-mates to appear in the 1981 film *Escape to Victory* and played the German goalkeeper, made 141 appearances for the club between 1969 and 1984.

At 5ft, 8in tall he was the shortest 'keeper in the entire Football League but also considered one of the bravest.

He once ended up with 11 stitches, lost a couple of teeth and suffered an horrendous black eye after bravely diving at the feet of Aston Villa centre forward Andy Gray.

His face was so disfigured that the *EADT* refused to print a photograph that was taken of him after the game!

Sivell thought he had made his farewell appearance for the club in a 2–0 defeat to Spurs the previous month, when he admitted he could have prevented both goals. So he was surprised when he arrived at Portman Road to be told he would be playing in a Tuesday night Division One league game against Southampton, because he did not know that regular 'keeper Paul Cooper had sustained a back injury.

It was to prove to be a night to forget for Sivell and Ipswich as they slumped to an embarrassing 3–0 defeat in front of their own fans.

The 33-year-old told me the following morning that he accepted responsibility for the Saints' opener but not the second and third goals, as the visitors romped into a three-goal lead inside 36 minutes.

Sivell had been on the receiving end of sarcastic jeers whenever he caught the ball during the second half.

Speaking from his home at North Cove, near Beccles, a distraught Sivell said: "I was rather disgusted by it, to be honest. I think the treatment I received from the fans was unwarranted. You can only go out and do your best.

"When the fans stoop to that level I think it is diabolical.

"Whatever the reasons of the fans, I still think they are ignorant to do that. I had hardly anything else to do."

Sivell even went so far as to say that he felt the understudy job should be given to either Gary Westwood or Youth team 'keeper Jon Hallworth, who was injured at the time.

Ipswich Town manager Bobby Ferguson said he felt sorry for Sivell and agreed it was a disgrace the way the crowd had treated him.

"He has come back while not quite fit, but I didn't blame him entirely for the defeat," he said.

Crocked Essex cricketer Robert Rollins was disappointed but remained philosophical when he spoke to me after seeing his career ended by injury in December 1999.

The 25-year-old wicket-keeper, who had been widely touted as a possible successor to Jack Russell behind the stumps for England, was forced to retire due to a serious knee injury.

It was a cruel end to a promising career that saw Rollins feature in just 69 first-class matches after making his debut in 1992.

Rollins, who conceded he was sometimes in such pain that he struggled to walk up the stairs, called time on his career after seeking the advice of a specialist.

He said: "I am disappointed, but it's not the end of the world. I loved playing cricket, but there are other things in life. I have got my medals and TV clips – I am happy with what I have achieved."

Rollins admitted he would have jumped at the chance to play international cricket.

"I would have loved to have done so. Not many people have the chance. I believe I got close a few times, but it was not to be," he said.

27. Rags, riches and regrets

EVEN now, 30 years later, it seems surreal.

How do you come to fall out with one of the nation's best-loved sportsmen?

You would have thought it hard to do.

But it happened to me and remains arguably the most bizarre incident during my entire career as a sports journalist.

The sportsman in question was Derek Randall, who played 47 Tests and 49 one-day internationals for England in the late 1970s and early 1980s.

The Nottinghamshire batsman is widely regarded as one of the best fielders ever to grace the game, as well as being an eccentric character.

Randall memorably doffed his cap in the direction of Dennis Lillee after narrowly evading a bouncer bowled by the Australian during the Centenary Test at Melbourne in 1977.

He allegedly told Lillee: "No point hitting me there mate, there's nothing in it."

After finally being dismissed for 174 Randall exited the MCG arena via the wrong gate and found himself climbing towards the Royal Enclosure where Queen Elizabeth II was watching, before being hastily redirected.

Randall is one of those chirpy chappies that everyone can relate to, and I was no different when he first signed for Minor Counties side Suffolk ahead of the 1994 season.

Nothing seemed too much trouble for 'Rags' as he posed for pictures and conducted interviews.

I interviewed him at the launch of Ipswich School's new indoor cricket centre and aboard a container ship prior to the start of the season at the announcement that the Medite Shipping Company were to be the county's new sponsors.

Then there was my brief interview with him as he lay in his sick bed before the second day's play of his Minor Counties Championship debut against Cumberland at Kendal.

But all that changed as the result of a story I wrote in the build-up to the two-day championship match at home to Bedfordshire in early July.

The irony behind our fall-out is that I had tried to help Randall be available for the fixture at the Ransomes Sports Ground in Ipswich.

I was approached by Tony Warrington, Suffolk's assistant secretary, a couple of weeks before the match asking for my assistance.

The match was originally scheduled for the Sunday and Monday, but the start was put back a day because Bedfordshire were involved in an MCC Trophy semi-final on the Sunday.

Randall, who had retired from first-class cricket the previous season, was working on a freelance basis for the *Worksop Guardian* covering a local cricket match on Saturdays and writing a weekly sports column.

As Randall himself told me in the *Evening Star* back-page story that appeared a week in advance of the match: "I was planning to play on the Sunday and Monday and write my sports column on the Tuesday.

"However, now the game has been moved to the Monday and Tuesday this is no longer possible."

It was because of this that Warrington enlisted my help by asking was there any way that Randall could come into our newspaper offices and write his column so that he could file his copy and also play in the match.

The question was raised with Mike Horne, the sports editor of the *Evening Star* at the time, and although the company were willing to help by allowing Randall to use a computer, it was not possible to transmit the copy across.

That may seem strange reading it now, but don't forget that this was way before email and the Internet became part and parcel of our daily working lives.

The bad news was relayed back to Randall, who I subsequently rang to obtain the above quotes for the aforementioned story.

Randall had already missed the match away to Staffordshire at Longton in early June due to a long-standing corporate hospitality commitment at his former home ground Trent Bridge for the England versus New Zealand Test.

Now the Ipswich public were to miss the opportunity to see him playing for Suffolk.

"I was really looking forward to playing against Bedfordshire," concluded Randall in my story.

Now so far as I was aware there was nothing contentious in what I had written, and I had provided a platform for Randall to give his side of the story before it was printed.

The story appeared under the headline 'Part-timer Randall can't play' and I can only assume that it was this that upset the ex-England international so much.

The phrase 'part-timer' referred to his working as a freelance writer, but perhaps Randall thought it implied he was playing part-time for Suffolk.

Randall appeared in all five of Suffolk's remaining championship fixtures, ending the season with 597 runs from 14 innings at an average of 42.64.

But he would not speak to me for the rest of the summer, even declining an interview on the final day of the season as Suffolk faced Norfolk at Copdock but happily speaking to David Cuffley, who was there covering the match for the *Eastern Daily Press*.

Any thoughts I entertained that a new season would see a thaw in our frosty relationship soon evaporated.

Randall had already missed an MCC Trophy first-round tie and two out of the three two-day championship fixtures of the 1995 campaign when Suffolk set off for Bristol to face Gloucestershire in the first round of the NatWest Trophy.

The squad stayed overnight in the city, but Randall did not arrive that evening as had been expected.

Randall was nowhere to be seen when the two teams had to be declared before the captains tossed up 20 minutes before the scheduled start of play the following morning.

So ex-Essex Second XI all-rounder Craig Miller was named in the Suffolk side instead of Randall, who then arrived at the County Ground ten minutes before play commenced at 10.30am.

I waited a while before leaving the Press Box and heading round towards the changing rooms to try to speak to Randall about his late arrival.

But he walked straight past me and headed for his car before driving off.

I was subsequently told that Randall had apparently left his Retford home at 7am after attending an engagement in Accrington the previous evening, but got stuck in traffic on the M42.

The following day's *EADT* carried the story that I filed which stated that Randall's future as Suffolk's professional looked increasingly unlikely to extend beyond his initial two-year contract with the county after this latest escapade.

He was again absent for the 10-wicket MCC Trophy quarter-final defeat away to Herefordshire, before featuring in all six remaining two-day fixtures.

A four-wicket loss to Norfolk in the final match ended Suffolk's dreams of winning the Eastern Division title, but Randall had redeemed himself in the eyes of the county's hierarchy.

He figured in seven of the nine two-day championship matches, scoring 727 runs in 13 innings at an average of 55.92.

Although I followed Suffolk's fortunes during the first half of the 1996 season, my elevation to the position of sports editor of the *EADT* meant I never covered any matches thereafter.

Randall surprised everyone by playing for Suffolk for a further five seasons, even staying on for the summer of 2000 after initially saying the previous year was to be his swansong.

By the time he retired – after hitting a season-high 75 in his 50th and final match in a rain-affected win against Norfolk – Randall had scored 3,935 runs for Suffolk at an average of 45.75, with eight centuries and 27 fifties.

And whatever the reason for our fall-out, 'Rags' had put it firmly behind him as he reflected on his seven-year love affair with Suffolk in an interview with me ahead of his last match.

He said: "I have probably enjoyed these past seven years more than when I was playing professional cricket as it has been more relaxed.

"My biggest disappointment over the seven years is that we have not got to a one-day Final at Lord's. That and the fact that I never really played a big innings to win a game."

28. Gaffes and guffaws

THREE goals in the first six minutes of extra-time meant there would be no need for penalties.

Thurlow Nunn League Division One Ipswich Wanderers had put up a gallant fight, but it was to no avail.

After holding Premier Division opponents Felixstowe & Walton United to 1–1 at the end of 90 minutes, Wanderers had been blown away at the start of extra-time by that three-goal blitz.

The closing stages of the Red Insure Cup first-round tie in October 2012 were going to be academic, and so I could start to draft out my report.

Jordan Matthews added a fine individual fifth goal early in the second period of extra-time and that was that – or so I thought.

I filed my report and went into the clubhouse at Wanderers' Humber Doucy Lane ground to get out of the cold and buy a drink.

While I was waiting for Kevin O'Donnell, the new Felixstowe & Walton United manager, to appear so that I could introduce myself and interview him, I got chatting in a group and said I felt the final 5–1 scoreline was harsh on Wanderers.

It was only when I was corrected that I realised I had committed one of the worst gaffes that a sports reporter can make – I had got the scoreline wrong!

While I was busy tapping away on my laptop Matt Buckle had scored a sixth goal for the Seasiders in the last minute and I had missed it.

There had not even been a ripple of applause to alert me, the goal having no bearing on the final outcome and most of the crowd of 81 had either gone home, were already in the bar or too cold to celebrate.

Fortunately I was able to ring through and get the scoreline changed and add that Buckle had completed the scoring at the end of my report before it was too late.

It was the only time that I ever filed a report with the wrong result, something even Sky Sports were guilty of in November 2009.

I was in the Press Room at the Weston Homes Community Stadium after watching Colchester United when, much to my surprise, *Gillette Soccer Saturday* presenter Jeff Stelling read out the result of a Ridgeons League game towards the end of the show.

I don't know whether I was more staggered that the Step 5 league should get a mention or the result of the Premier Division match between Haverhill Rovers and Wivenhoe Town.

Surely I hadn't heard that right? Haverhill Rovers 9 Wivenhoe 9. But then I must have done, otherwise why would it have been picked up and broadcast on the show?

But my disbelief was based on the fact that Wivenhoe, who were rock bottom of the table at the time with only one point, had found the net just seven times in 15 league games prior to kick-off.

I logged straight on to first the *Green 'Un* and then the Ridgeons League websites as soon as I got home and, sure enough, it was a bogus scoreline.

The match had, in fact, been postponed, but I was still intrigued as to how the result came to be broadcast as a 9–9 draw.

I rang the Sky Sports Press Office before writing my weekly 'Scene & Heard' blog for the *Green 'Un* website, to be told that it was a case of human error.

I was informed that Sky are fed the scorelines from the Press Association and that whoever typed in the result at PA had keyed in 9–9 rather than pp!

So 18 goals were 'scored' in a game that never even took place!

Getting the wrong goalscorer is an occupational hazard for any sports journalist, and something I have been guilty of on the odd occasion.

It was on the same Ipswich Wanderers ground that I was guilty of such a gaffe 18 months after that game against Felixstowe, although by then I was no longer working for Archant Ltd but in my present role with Suffolk FA.

The Sunday Cup Final was one of those games that had everything – ten goals, a penalty and a sending off.

What's more Gym United striker Andrew Wood netted all six of his side's goals in their 6–4 victory over Kitchener Taverners. Or that's what I thought and had tweeted during the match.

After photographing the presentation ceremony on the pitch I grabbed two of the match balls from the officials as I thought a photograph of Wood holding them to celebrate his double hat-trick would be the perfect picture to accompany an interview.

I got Wood to hold one ball in the palm of each hand and snapped the photograph before interviewing him.

Had the striker, who played for Walsham-le-Willows in the Premier Division of the Thurlow Nunn League on Saturdays, ever scored six times in a match before, I enquired?

"I once scored 11 goals in one game and six in a Cup Final last season when we won 11–0. But today was ridiculous. You dream about winning the cup, but not about scoring like that in the Final," he replied.

Interview in the bag I went inside the clubhouse in search of winning manager Matt Morton, son of former Football League referee Kelvin Morton.

It was only in the course of conversation with Morton Junior when I mentioned Wood scoring six that both he and Wayne Proctor, Wood's striker partner, convinced me that Proctor netted one of the goals that I had credited to Wood.

I was still tweeting that Wood had put Gym United 3–1 ahead after 33 minutes when the fourth goal went in, looked up, saw Wood running away celebrating and assumed (cardinal sin) that he had just scored his fourth.

So convinced was I that it was his goal that I had not felt the need to check with anyone else, and my error only came to light afterwards.

Which left me scratching my head as to why Wood had not questioned the use of two footballs to signify two hat-tricks or corrected me when I quizzed him about scoring six goals.

Fortunately, I was able to correct my copy before uploading it on the Suffolk FA website and distributing it to the local media.

Getting the wrong goalscorer is bad enough, but interviewing the wrong person is arguably even worse!

I had met Dereham Town manager Matt Henman at the start of the 2012–13 season, introducing myself to him before the Magpies' home match at Aldiss Park against Brantham Athletic in the Thurlow Nunn League.

Fast forward to the following February at Notcutts Park and I saw what I thought was Henman walk into the bar area following Dereham's 3–1 win.

It was only when we sat down at a nearby table that I realised that it was not Henman that I was about to interview, but his assistant Neal Simmons!

I was too embarrassed to admit that I thought he was Henman and so went ahead and interviewed him instead!

All journalists make mistakes – they are human after all – but when they end up in print they are there in black and white for all to see. I once committed the same error twice in the same week, after convincing myself that Fareham was in Kent, after confusing the Hampshire town with Farnham!

Some mistakes are blatantly obvious, others not so, and some just leap off the page at you.

Not a mistake as such, but the headline on the front page of the *Evening Star* following a sizzling day at the annual Suffolk Show had to be hurriedly changed between editions after no-one spotted it before the Presses rolled. It simply said:

PHEW
IT'S A
SHOW
SCORCHER

We all had a laugh about it later, but I don't know how many members of the public spotted it and thought the newspaper was taking the proverbial.

29. Stockings and suspenders

WE HAVE all made decisions in life that have come back to haunt us.

Whether it is just getting carried away on a wave of emotion or simply not thinking something through logically, on hindsight it has proven not to be such a good idea.

The idea of superimposing the face of a local celebrity onto a woman's body wearing stockings and suspenders and printing the image in a daily newspaper was ill-judged to say the least.

To this day it still ranks as the most gross error of judgement I have ever made in my professional career.

That I was not solely responsible does not alter the fact that I should have known better.

The fact that the person in question was none other than the then manager of Ipswich Town only exacerbated my embarrassment.

As is so often the case, it was one of those things that seemed like a good idea at the time, but in the cold light of day, well...

My *EADT* colleague Derek Davis had written a light-hearted article referring to Ipswich Town boss Joe Royle and his assistant Willie Donachie as *The Odd Couple* which was the name of an American TV Comedy.

The Odd Couple was about two men who lived together whose different lifestyles led to conflicts and laughs.

Royle and Donachie were at the time living together, after moving to Ipswich following Royle's appointment as manager in October 2002.

Paul Nixon, the head of photographic on the *EADT*, played

around with photoshop on his computer and created an image of Royle in stockings and suspenders.

Of course, the sight of such an image cause everyone who saw it to have a fit of the giggles – and that's where it should have ended.

But we – editor Terry Hunt, Nixon and myself – decided to use it on the sports pages in that Saturday's edition of the *EADT*, although as Friday unfolded stories were jostling for space and it was in danger of being squeezed out.

The only space left where we could possibly use it was as part of a popular and well-read fan's column written by my colleague Steve Mellen, without doubt one of the best writers I ever worked with.

When Mellen, who was on an evening subbing shift, arrived in the office in the late afternoon to be told the image was to be used in his column he was, understandably, non-plussed.

After all, it was not his idea and the offending image had nothing to do with what he would be writing about, but it was to appear under his name, and he was quite rightly absolved from any blame for what happened. The s**t, not surprisingly, hit the fan after the offending image appeared in print the following day, with Hunt having to pacify the club and apologise.

It was all the more unfortunate and inappropriate as Royle was one of the most media-savvy managers around and enjoyed a good relationship with the local media.

He was almost always available and supplied a constant source of stories for my colleagues Davis, Dave Allard, Mel Henderson and Elvin King.

But he loathed letters pages and radio phone-ins with a passion. We knew this when he arrived at Ipswich, following fall-outs with the local media during his time as manager at Everton.

Royle felt it unfair that correspondents – some of whom had not even attended matches – could have their say in the local press or on radio stations.

Although you could understand his frustration at some of what was said about him and his team, the other side of the argument is the freedom of speech which exists in this country.

Either way, so hot under the collar did Royle get that I recall being summoned – the only time I have ever been inside the Ipswich Town manager's office – to Portman Road along with Hunt.

He told us in no uncertain terms how he felt the negative mood of correspondents in the letters' columns in the *EADT* was undermining his attempt to steer Ipswich Town to play-off success.

Fall-outs with local football clubs are part and parcel of provincial journalism, and it is sometimes a fine line between being supportive and being critical when you are dealing with a club on a daily basis.

I had a fall-out with Wivenhoe Town after I criticised the club's facilities in my weekly 'Scene & Heard' blog I wrote on the *Green 'Un* website and also AFC Sudbury over a story following the release of several players, but both soon blew over.

However, I literally found myself backed into a corner when some of Suffolk's players took exception to an article I wrote in my weekly cricket column in the *Evening Star* during the 1993 season.

Each week I wrote a comment piece under the banner 'Playing Straight' – an opinion piece which tackled topical cricketing issues.

In the early season matches I had noticed that the contingent of former Essex players in the Suffolk side – skipper Ray East plus Adrian Brown, Keith Butler, Andrew Golding and Craig Miller – were wearing an assortment of Essex caps and sweaters, even though they were representing Suffolk.

Not only did the team look like a motley crew but I felt they were being disrespectful to Suffolk by appearing in Essex gear, even though none of them were still associated with the first-class county.

What's more, I remarked, with Suffolk due to host Essex in the first round of the NatWest Trophy at Bury St Edmunds that summer, the large crowd that was anticipated may think they were watching Essex playing against Essex Second XI!

The comment did not go down well and slow left-armer Andrew Golding, once seen as Ray East's successor at Essex, refused to speak to me after claiming match figures of 10 for 78 against Hertfordshire at Stowmarket.

The situation was arguably exacerbated by my colleague Martin White's very clever 'Silence is Golding' headline in the following day's *Evening Star*, after hearing how I had been shunned.

Matters reached a head when Suffolk faced Bedfordshire at Henlow just over a week before the showpiece occasion, some of the former Essex players rounding on me in the pub.

Although outnumbered I defended my comments, despite the players saying that they wore their Essex caps as some of them had not been capped by Suffolk and therefore did not possess the correct caps and they had to buy jumpers from the county and didn't see why they should, or had just not got round to doing so.

Suffice to say that when they took to the field in front of a near 4,000 crowd at the Victory Ground they were all correctly kitted out in Suffolk gear.

Part Seven
– Well I never

30. *That really did happen*

IMAGINE a Test umpire taking the players back out onto the field because a tea lady said she was not ready!

The incident really did occur in a NatWest Trophy first-round match between Suffolk and Northamptonshire at Bury St Edmunds in June 1989.

Northants had batted first and were fielding in Suffolk's reply when John Holder, who had officiated in the first of his 11 Test matches a year before, and fellow umpire Bob Duckett took the players off for tea.

Suffolk opening bowler Hedley Wright recalled: "Northants came off for tea and (Northants skipper) Allan Lamb led the players into the pavilion.

"Pat Coates looked at Allan Lamb and he looked back at her so she said 'what do you want?' because no-one had told her what time tea was supposed to be!

"I think John Holder then came up and Pat said 'you had better go out and carry on playing until tea is ready' so off they went!"

Pat subsequently told me that it was not the umpires but Lamb who made the decision to go back out.

A rain interruption had resulted in confusion over the time that tea was to be taken, and England batsman Lamb duly led his players back out for a few more overs until Pat and her colleagues were ready.

Incidentally, the loss of overs due to the rain meant the match spilled over into a second day, when Lamb and fellow England cricketer Greg Thomas took the tea ladies into town to help buy lunch to be served in the pavilion.

Lamb also bought a big bouquet of flowers on behalf of the Northants team as a thank you for the way they had been looked after.

As for me, I was banned from entering the pavilion for the following two seasons by Pat for the way I reported the tea-delay incident in the next day's *EADT!* An equally bizarre incident that I reported on while covering Suffolk occurred during the Minor Counties Championship match against Northumberland at Jesmond in 1993.

In those days championship matches were two-day games and when Suffolk batsman Mick Peck walked to the wicket on the second morning I had no idea what was about to happen.

Peck had been batting for around 15 minutes when Northumberland opening bowler Graeme Angus fired in a short delivery that appeared to shake up Peck.

As Angus approached the crease again Peck pulled away and he appeared to start shaking. The Suffolk batsman's legs then gave way as he collapsed in a heap.

Assistance was called for from the pavilion and then an ambulance was summoned and drove onto the pitch and out to the wicket.

All this was unfolding before my eyes just before I was due to file my lunchtime copy on the morning's play.

I had no idea what had happened to Peck and had to choose my words carefully to describe the events unfolding before me, ensuring I neither over-dramatised nor trivialised events.

Peck spent the afternoon in hospital under observation before being released later that day.

Unbeknown to me he had accompanied team-mate Robert Gregg to casualty the night before after Gregg had been involved in a fight with team-mate Keith 'Billy' Butler.

Peck had drunk plenty of caffeine to help him stay awake and when he went out to bat he had suffered an Epileptic fit.

Peck's collapse was much like Suffolk's entire batting line-up in the first innings when they were dismissed for a paltry 88.

The official scorecard recorded: 'M.J. Peck retired ill 8' in Suffolk's second innings as the hosts romped to a six-wicket win.

Suffolk were involved in another bizarre occurrence in an MCCA Knock-out tie against Lincolnshire at Framlingham College in June 1990.

The hosts were bowled out for 201, but only 2.3 overs into the visitors' reply the heavens opened and persistent drizzle forced the match to be abandoned.

A ten overs-a-side match was then started, but this, too, was abandoned after just three overs had been bowled.

Under the rules of the competition a toss of the coin was the only option available to settle the outcome other than a bowling at the stumps decider.

So with conditions too wet outside, the action moved indoors and, more precisely, into the college's sports hall situated just behind the cricket pavilion.

Tables which had been left set out neatly in rows for GCSE examinations the following day were moved aside and a matting wicket was laid out.

Five players from each side were nominated to bowl twice each at the stumps, with Lincolnshire winning 3–2, before going on to reach the final at Lord's for the first time in their history!

Jon Zagni had never before claimed a championship wicket for Suffolk in the 52 overs of slow left arm he had sent down for the county after making his debut in 1988.

But that all changed in the course of one afternoon at Copdock in the final match of the 1992 season against old rivals Norfolk.

The first session of the first-ever Minor Counties match to be staged at the ground was lost to the weather.

When play did get under way the cavalier approach adopted by both teams in the quest to secure as many first innings points as possible certainly made up for the delayed start.

A bemused Zagni was the main beneficiary, claiming seven of the nine wickets to fall, and, not quite so surprisingly, both teams did enough to qualify for the NatWest Trophy the following season.

Let's just say that had it been a horse race there may well have been a steward's enquiry!

The same could be said about the amount of injury time played at Chadfields, the home of Tilbury FC, on an unforgettable night in May 2012.

The wettest end to a football season in recent memory meant that the Ryman League Division One North play-off semi-final between the Dockers and Needham Market had already been postponed three times.

The tie had originally been scheduled for the previous Tuesday, but was given the go-ahead for the Friday night, which was just as well as the Final was taking place on the Sunday afternoon.

Tilbury took the lead after just six minutes but Needham were level four minutes before the break, Sam Newson converting a penalty.

Duane Wright put Needham ahead just seconds after coming on as a 72nd minute substitute.

The heavy pitch then began to take its toll as players started to go down with cramp and other injures.

The 90 minute mark came and went with Needham still leading 2–1, but Tilbury incredibly equalised in the 13th minute of injury time through Eljay Worrell.

A further five minutes passed before the full-time whistle blew with the sides locked at 2–2 and so after 118 minutes of play it was to be extra-time.

Jack West put the Dockers in front five minutes into the first period of extra-time, before Newson, who had struggled to score in open play in the second half of the season after suffering a knee ligament injury in December, equalised just before half-time of extra-time.

Newson then netted the winner in the last minute of extra-time to complete his hat-trick and conclude a tie that, by my calculations, had lasted an incredible 153 minutes!

With the deadline for the first edition of the *EADT* only ten minutes away, it had been quicker for me to dictate a few paragraphs to say the match was entering extra-time than to send copy via my laptop.

Now, while the drama in the stands didn't quite match that out on the pitch, as I started to file my final report, the battery on my laptop (there was no plug in the antiquated wooden stand to attach it to) decided it was as drained as everyone else and died on me.

So I was back on the phone to sub-editor Mike Cracknell to dictate the outcome of this remarkable match, the official 'deadline' having already passed for the second edition of the *EADT* so late did the match finish.

As the players trooped off the pitch it was fast approaching 11pm and Needham had to travel home, before heading back down the A12 on Sunday morning for the Final.

There was to be no fairytale ending as Enfield, who enjoyed home advantage as well as an extra day's rest after winning their semi-final on penalties on the Thursday night, won 1–0.

31. You couldn't make it up!

ALESSANDRO Zarrelli. The name sounds like that of an Italian international footballer, although it meant nothing to me the first time I heard it mentioned. That was during a phone call I received from Maurice Scrivener, the registrations and records officer of the Ridgeons League, in early December in 2011.

Maurice was ringing to tell me that Zarrelli, a 27-year-old Italian, had signed for two of the league's clubs – Norwich United and Ipswich Wanderers – simultaneously.

This was clearly a breach of league rules and Maurice thought I may be interested in learning more about Zarrelli's background with a view to doing a story.

"Type his name into Google and see what comes up," he said.

Sure enough, there were several articles on Alessandro Zarrelli, the most eye-catching of which was that he had been exposed in the Sky TV documentary *Superfakes*.

Zarrelli was exposed as living a Walter Mitty style existence, claiming to have been contracted to professional clubs Glasgow Rangers and Sheffield Wednesday and on-loan to MK Dons, before admitting there was not a shred of truth to what he had said.

He had played for a string of clubs, including teams in Ireland and Wales in 2005 and 2006, after allegedly making the same false claims, before turning out for Hucknall Town.

Zarrelli then signed for Norwich United on 5 November 2011, giving his address as 401, Carrow Road in Norwich – an address that didn't even exist.

Just six days later he was sent off in his one and only appearance for the club's reserve side for foul and abusive language and banned for two matches.

On 29 November he signed a registration form with a view to joining Ipswich Wanderers, even though his suspension was due to start on 2 December.

It was then that Scrivener contacted me, and over the course of the next fortnight the further I delved into the story, the more it fascinated me.

I rang Zarrelli to speak to him, but once he realised I was a journalist, he denied it was him answering his own mobile phone, even though I knew I had the right number!

I subsequently spoke to his legal representative, who specialised in reputation management and who initially warned me to be very careful about writing anything to do with his client.

However, after subsequently contacting him a second time and presenting all the facts, he was more forthcoming about me speaking to Zarrelli.

Strangely, when I again rang the number I had previously called, Zarrelli again answered his own phone and this time spoke to me.

He went on to claim there had been a 'misunderstanding' and denied any wrong doing in registering for two clubs simultaneously.

The story, which had involved more checking by the newspaper's legal firm than any other I wrote, was given the go-ahead to be published.

Zarrelli subsequently played for Diss Town, Downham Town and Long Melford in the Ridgeons League without making anywhere near the same impact on the field as he had off it.

That conveniently brings me on to another story you couldn't make up involving Ipswich and Norwich.

The story concerned a striker from Ipswich scoring a hat-trick on the last day of the season to save Norwich from relegation!

There's a saying that fact is stranger than fiction – and it certainly was in the case of 28-year-old Keith Hetherington in May 2009.

The Ipswich-based striker netted a hat-trick for Norwich United to save the mustard city side from dropping out of the Ridgeons League Premier Division.

His treble enabled Norwich United to beat Histon Reserves 3–1 and clamber out of the bottom two on the final day of the season thanks to Woodbridge Town also defeating Harwich & Parkeston, who finished second bottom instead.

Ironically, the Shrimpers were spared relegation due to the fact that Premier Division winners Lowestoft Town were promoted.

However, their reprieve was short-lived – the Shrimpers withdrew from the league the following February.

Goalkeeper Andrew Plummer was also a match-winner but at both ends of the pitch in a Ryman League Cup tie in November 2011.

The former Ipswich Town apprentice joined Needham Market at the start of the 2011–12 season, after spending two-and-half years playing for Glenavon in Northern Ireland.

Needham were trailing 3–2 at Concord Rangers in the Alan Boon Cup when Plummer headed home at the far post in the fourth and last minute of added time to equalise.

With no extra-time played in the competition, it was straight to a penalty shoot-out.

Concord scored their first spot kick but the second went over the crossbar, before Plummer then saved the next two to seal a 3–1 success and secure a place in the third round.

The 22-year-old, who used to play in goal and on pitch as a midfielder or striker in his youth, said: "It was the sort of stuff you dream about. It was a great night."

Ipswich referee Les King was also in dreamland when he received a letter stating he had been shortlisted to officiate at the London 2012 Olympic Games.

King received a letter earlier that year which he thought was an official invitation, even though he was just a Level 5 referee who officiated in the Kent Blaxill Border League and Ridgeons Youth League, as well as in schools' and youth matches.

Part of the letter stated: "It gives me the greatest pleasure to advise you that because of your dedication, honest, unfailing and continued efforts as a senior amateur referee, you have been selected to join a shortlist of candidates to participate in one or more of the Men's or Women's football ties as the match referee or referee's assistant."

Enclosed in the letter was a stamped addressed envelope to return to the Eastern Region Area Selection Committee for the Olympics Football based at Writtle, near Chelmsford.

King said he had started to fill out the form and it was only when he came to the section which said 'Are you in receipt of any state benefit or pension?' that he realised he had been duped.

He told me: "I realised it was a scam as it was just before my 65th birthday! I was really taken in by it, and word has since got around and local referees know about it."

32. Strange but true

SUFFOLK cricketer Tom Huggins thought it was a wind-up when he received a voicemail asking him to ring TalkSPORT radio.

The Bury St Edmunds skipper, not adverse to a practical joke himself, ignored the message and it was only a couple of days later when the radio station rang again that he realised it was for real.

TalkSPORT were chasing Huggins for an interview after reading my story in the *EADT* that he had taken five wickets in five balls in a T20 competition.

Huggins, who was subsequently interviewed by the station, admitted to me he had not appreciated the magnitude of what he had achieved at the time.

Cambridge Granta had reached 132 for 3 chasing Bury's total of 165 in the Gibbs Denley East Anglian Premier League T20 competition before Huggins intervened.

His five wickets from consecutive deliveries saw him finish with figures of 4-0-20-6 as Bury won by 13 runs.

However, Huggins revealed: "I came off not realising I had taken five in five because the first wicket was with the last ball of the previous over!"

Opening batsman Robbie Barber achieved an equally astounding cricketing feat when he struck 40 runs off one over at Braintree's Panfield Lane ground.

The 29-year-old Maldon skipper was playing in a Two Counties Championship Senior Cup match in July 2000 when he carted Steve Hale to all corners.

The first delivery went for six over mid-wicket, the second – a no-ball – went for six over square leg, the third for four through mid-wicket, the fourth for six over long on, the fifth for six over mid-wicket and both the sixth and seventh for sixes over square leg.

Barber reflected: "It was an interesting over! To be perfectly honest, the ball I hit for four should have gone for six as well, but I didn't strike it cleanly and it bounced just inside the boundary.

"I have no idea how many balls were lost – the umpire just kept getting another one out of his pocket."

Barber's pyrotechnics ultimately counted for nothing as the match was washed out after he had smashed 71 off just 27 balls.

Panfield Lane was also the scene of another strange but true cricketing story, when Braintree Second XI captain Geoff Eveling only realised he had scored his maiden century in the bar after the game!

The 30-year-old thought he had been left stranded on 99 not out for the second time in his career in a 222-run demolition of Ipswich-based side DBSL (an acronym for Deep Backward Square Leg) in a Two Counties Division Six match in June 2009.

Eveling added 238 with Rory Ainsley, who scored 134, in an undefeated second-wicket stand. But it was only when he checked the scorebook in the bar afterwards that he realised he had reached three figures for the first time in his career.

He said: "The original scores did not add up properly, so I then had to ask someone else to check that I was not having a laugh with myself!"

Eveling, who had been playing cricket since the age of 14, was left stranded on 99 not out in a tour match a few years previously.

"I had better score another one so I can celebrate properly," said the man christened Geoff after Geoff Boycott.

Leiston footballer Leon Ottley-Gooch certainly had cause for celebration after predicting he would score a hat-trick before one of the biggest games of his career.

His treble helped Leiston clinch promotion from Ryman League Division One North at the first attempt in May 2012 following promotion from the Ridgeons League 12 month earlier.

Ottley-Gooch scored three times in six second-half minutes – the first hat-trick of his senior career – as Leiston overpowered Potters Bar 6–0 to clinch the title.

He told me afterwards: "I can't quite believe it – I am completely lost for words. Before the game I was really buzzing in the changing room and I was so up for it that I said I was going to get a hat-trick."

Ottley-Gooch's other claim to fame is that he is related to Nicola Adams, who won gold in the women's boxing at the London 2012 Olympics.

Nicola, who is his auntie's daughter on his father's side of the family, subsequently appeared alongside Ottley-Gooch on the hit TV show *Family Fortunes*.

Another strange but true tale was Ian Booth's visit to a cemetery that inspired him to become his cricket club's all-time record appearance-maker.

The St Margaret's all-rounder had been retired for a couple of seasons due to a knee injury.

He revealed: "I was visiting the cemetery when I came across a memorial for Richard Robinson, the former Suffolk all-rounder, and I thought how he would love to still be playing cricket now.

"That made my mind up to start playing again. My knee improved and I got myself fitter and started playing once more."

Around ten years later Booth, who by then had celebrated his 50th birthday, became the Ipswich club's record appearance-maker, playing his 551st match for the Saints at home to Long Melford in June 2010.

Luke Ingram possibly set an appearance record of a different kind when he played for three different football clubs in three different competitions in one week!

It was in February 2012 that Ingram, who was 19 at the time, produced his three-club trick.

He turned out for Hadleigh United, where he was on loan, in a Ridgeons League fixture on the Saturday, before coming on as a substitute for parent club Bury Town against Needham Market in a Suffolk FA Premier Cup tie the following Tuesday.

AFC Sudbury then stepped in to take Ingram on loan, and he made his debut for the Ryman League Division One North side at home to Leiston the following Saturday!

Promising player Oliver Hammond would have been grateful to make even a single appearance for one club on the bowls green in the summer of 2009.

The 14-year-old's feet were so big – a whopping size 14 – that he couldn't find any bowls shoes to fit him.

Without the correct footwear his club would not risk picking him for league matches for fear of being unable to play him.

The 6ft, 1in tall teenager, who was the youngest member of The Woolpack Bowls Club in Ipswich, said: "It is frustrating that I can't play in the league, but because I can't find any bowls shoes to fit me we decided it was best I don't play because of the possibility that teams might object to me not having the right footwear."

Strange but true indeed.

33. Right time, right place

SAM Newson had been on fire, scoring 29 goals including 21 in the league to shoot Needham Market to the top of the Ryman League Division One North table in December 2011.

His goalscoring exploits, not surprisingly, had brought him to the attention of a bevy of potential suitors and had landed him a trial at Gillingham.

The trial was due to start on the Monday after that Saturday's game against Kent visitors Chatham Town, ironically a side from the same county as the League Two side.

With Needham trailing 1–0 and just 15 minutes remaining, Newson chased a through ball and went down as he was challenged by visiting keeper Tim Roberts.

The longer he stayed down the more apparent it became that the injury was serious, and a stretcher was called.

Chatham hung on to win the match and so end the Suffolk side's undefeated home record, but the repercussions were more far reaching for Newson.

The 23-year-old striker's left knee was, as he put it, 'the size of a small child's head' and there was no way he would be travelling down to Gillingham on the Sunday night.

Newson, who later left the ground on crutches, admitted he was 'gutted' by his bad luck.

He told me: "I have had so many tweets from Gillingham fans wishing me well and saying they hope I get better soon so I can go down there on trial in the near future."

Unfortunately Newson was never invited back, but his bad luck was my good fortune in terms of being in the right place at the right time, to land the story of how his big chance had been cruelly wrecked by injury.

A similar fate befell Ollie Mann, the striker who succeeded Newson as the top scorer in the Ridgeons League, Newson having led the end-of-season goalscoring charts while with Stanway Rovers prior to joining Needham.

Mann was starting to attract the attention of several Football League clubs due to his exploits at Brantham Athletic.

The season after topping the Division One list as Brantham won promotion, Mann did the same in the Premier Division, bagging an impressive 41 goals.

The following season the goals were still going in and it appeared only a matter of time before a higher-league club made their move.

I was surprised to see Mann in the clubhouse half-an-hour before kick-off when I turned up at Notcutts Park, home of Woodbridge Town, for a Wednesday night fixture against Brantham Athletic in September 2011.

When I enquired as to why he wasn't playing, I quickly realised I had stumbled across a good story.

The previous Monday he had started what was due to be a week-long trial at League One Colchester United.

However, just half-an-hour in to what he hoped would be his big break, Mann was injured in a tackle.

He had taken a blow on his left knee, the same one he had an operation on at the end of the 2009–10 season.

Mann, who had turned 22 earlier that month, said: "There was some contact and I went down like a sack of potatoes. I could not play on any more, so I had some lunch and some treatment before going home."

Unfortunately for both Mann and Newson their respective injuries scuppered their trials and opportunity never knocked again.

It was at Notcutts Park in February 2013 that I picked up a story purely by chance, although I must confess I nearly missed it.

I had gone along to cover Woodbridge Town's home game against Dereham Town for no other reason than it had been a while since the Woodpeckers had been picked as the main match for Monday's coverage in the *EADT* and *Ipswich Star* and they were facing the title challengers.

Dereham coasted to a 3–1 victory and it was while interviewing Woodbridge manager Mark Scopes afterwards that my ears suddenly pricked up.

Scopes revealed the club were suffering a 'short-term cash flow problem' as a result of the recent bout of bad weather.

"I called a meeting with the players on Wednesday night and told them they will not get paid this month, may not get paid next month and may not even get paid again this season," said Scopes.

He assumed that I had got wind of what had happened and that was why I was there to cover the game, but had he not mentioned the club's plight I may well have left the ground blissfully unaware of the financial crisis.

The same could be said of my interview with FC Clacton manager David Coyle, after seeing his side lift the Ridgeons League Division One KO Cup in May 2010.

I was interviewing Coyle, whose side had just defeated Halstead Town 2–1 in the final of a competition which normally the *EADT* would have asked a freelance to cover on our behalf.

However, I volunteered to go along and cover the Friday night Final – and was rewarded with a scoop, after FC Clacton had added the cup to winning promotion to the Premier Division.

While his players were celebrating their double success next door in the bar, Coyle revealed he would not be in charge the following season.

He said: "I made my mind up two or three weeks ago, but I haven't told the players yet. I could not bring myself to tell them tonight because they are enjoying their success."

Success went hand-in-hand with Suffolk boxer David Starie throughout his career all the way to two world title fights.

Starie fought, and lost, to both Joe Calzaghe and Steve Ottke on points in his two super middleweight world title bouts, but both of those were a far cry from the night I was the only journalist present to see him in his very first fight as a 12-year-old.

Ironically, the Ipswich Greyfriars Round Table Amateur Boxing Evening at the Moat House on the outskirts of Ipswich was the only such event I ever attended.

I was only there because Dave Allard, the regular *EADT* boxing correspondent at the time in October 1986, was away in Hull, where Ipswich Town were playing the following afternoon.

'David Starie, 12, steals the show' was the headline in the *EADT*, after Starie came from behind in the first bout of the evening to score a unanimous victory.

His performance was so impressive it earned him the Fred Kay Memorial Shield – and a star-in-the-making was born.

One of the better news stories I wrote – it actually made the front page of the *EADT* – was while I was a trainee journalist working in Bury St Edmunds.

While having my haircut I got talking to my hairdresser about her boyfriend being suspended from the police force while an investigation was carried out after he was sent off in a five-a-side football tournament.

Had I used a different hairdresser or even had my hair cut a couple of weeks earlier or later, I may well not have stumbled across that particular story.

Definitely a case of being in the right place at the right time.

Part Eight
– View from the top

34. Grounds for concern

WHITTON United boss Ian Brown admitted he was so disappointed that he had seriously considered his future in football.

Brown had played professionally for Birmingham City, Bristol City, Colchester United and Northampton Town.

He then appeared for a whole host of non-league sides in Suffolk and Essex, including Braintree Town, Chelmsford City, Clacton Town, Felixstowe Town, Harwich & Parkeston, Maldon Town, Sudbury Town, Stowmarket Town, Whitton United and Witham Town.

But the 45-year-old was really down in the dumps after the Ipswich-based club's failure to win promotion from Division One of the Ridgeons League at the end of the 2010–11 season.

A tremendous run had seen the club finish runners-up – a single point behind champions Gorleston and five points clear of third-placed Diss Town.

The reason Whitton would not be playing Premier Division football the following season was down to the fact that a new £30,000 stand was not built in time.

A disillusioned Brown said: "I don't wish to get drawn into the politics of what happened – I will leave that to other people in the club – but I was left feeling sick to the stomach by the outcome.

"I was so disappointed by it all that I seriously considered my future in football, but I have tried to be positive and move on."

Work had started on the 113-seat stand in March, at which stage Whitton were outsiders to finish in the top three promotion places.

In order to be eligible for promotion the stand at their King

George V ground needed to be completed by the extended deadline date of 25 June – the day of the league's AGM.

The stand was key to the ground improvements the club was asked to carry out by league officials.

Whitton, who had withdrawn from the Premier Division in mid-season two years previously, were also told that if they finished in one of the promotion places they would have to appear before the league's management committee to convince them they would not pull out again.

Club chairman Ruel Fox, the former Norwich City, Newcastle United and Tottenham Hotspur winger, and secretary Phil Pemberton had given a presentation to the league, who were going to recommend Whitton be promoted.

However, the day before the AGM Peter Hutchings, the league's grounds standards officer, visited to check everything was in order.

Pemberton recalled: "He took one look at the stand and said he could not recommend our promotion to the league's management committee because the stand was not completed."

Whitton then withdrew their application, leaving Brown to consider his future.

He decided to stay on, and the club retained the Suffolk FA Senior Cup before he then left.

It was to be another two years at the end of the 2013–14 season that Whitton won promotion as champions and returned to the top flight of what was by then known as the Thurlow Nunn League.

I was called a K**bhead, it was suggested that I should be flogged on the centre circle and there were calls for me to be banned from the ground after a piece I wrote about Broad Lane, home of Wivenhoe Town.

The article appeared under the headline 'It doesn't get much worse than this' in my weekly Scene & Heard' blog on the *Green 'Un* website.

I expressed my views after my visit to watch the Dragons in a midweek Ridgeons League fixture in January 2010.

'From the moment I arrived in the pot-holed car park for the Premier Division match against Hadleigh United to when I left three hours later, I found the whole evening a rather depressing experience.

'It is hard to believe that Wivenhoe were once one of the region's top sides, punching above their weight as they did for several years in the Isthmian League,' I wrote.

Wivenhoe, a small village just outside Colchester, had indeed been one of the region's most successful sides and had attracted a string of ex-pros.

Goalkeeper Tony Godden, who was between the posts for the Baggies when Ipswich Town beat West Bromwich Albion in the FA Cup semi-final in 1978, Paul Price and John Lacy, both ex-Tottenham Hotspur defenders, and Lil Fuccillo, previously of Luton Town, were among those to strut their stuff at Broad Lane.

The blog stated that upon my arrival 45 minutes before kick-off the clubhouse was still in darkness, meaning that I had to ask someone if it was actually open.

And when I enquired of the gateman where the teams would be posted up before the match, so I could check the line-ups ahead of covering the match, I was told they would not be and nor was there to be an announcement made over the Tannoy prior to kick-off.

There then followed what I described as arguably the worst half of Ridgeons League Premier Division football I had witnessed on a dreadful surface, which included what amounted to a sandpit in one area of the pitch, although I admitted the near-freezing conditions didn't help.

The second half was an improvement – it couldn't have really failed to be – but the game still ended in an inevitable goalless draw before I was put out of my misery.

'Wivenhoe are second bottom of the table for a reason – the club have no cash and are asking boys to do a man's job at this level. And, to be fair to them, they deserved to defeat a very poor Hadleigh United on the night.

'It was only a lack of composure in front of goal and visiting goal-keeper Arron Benstead, that prevented the Dragons from recording just their second league win of the season,' I wrote.

Talk about stirring up a hornet's nest! I was Public Enemy No.1 in Wivenhoe over the next few days.

My comments were described as being 'negative', 'one-dimensional' and 'offensive' on the club's own website.

But on other forums some of my detractors really let rip.

Suffice to say I stood by my comments in the follow-up article I wrote and still do to this day.

Groundsmen often go to extraordinary lengths to get games on despite concerns about the weather, and sometimes their efforts are rewarded.

One such case was Brantham Athletic groundsman Allan Clarke, who battled all week in a bid to get the club's pitch fit for their FA Vase fourth round proper tie against Whitley Bay in January 2013.

Clarke got together a working party of nearly 30 people on the Wednesday evening and they spent more than three hours clearing snow off the pitch at Brantham Leisure Centre.

He said: "We were having a pitch inspection at 2pm on the Thursday, and if we had left the snow on, it would have failed because the pitch was judged on what the referee saw."

Clarke, who was also the club's vice-chairman at the time, spent an anxious night before the match praying the weather would not take a turn for the worse.

"We had committed ourselves to getting the game on, and with people travelling 300 miles, if it had been called off, I felt it would have been my fault."

Clarke was awake at 2.30am on the Saturday and looking out of his bedroom window waiting to see if the snow would return, before going down to the ground two hours later to aerate the pitch, which was still icy, and re-mark it.

His efforts were rewarded as Brantham beat four-time winners Whitley Bay 1–0 after extra time, thanks to a Dave Grimwood goal, to book their place in the last 16 of the competition.

Another groundsman with the surname Clarke gave Ipswich Cricket Club grounds for concern of a different type altogether.

Kester Clarke won the Terrain Aeriation Unsung Groundsman 2007 award in recognition of his outstanding performance and dedication to the club and the industry.

The award came just four years after Browns and Tattingstone cricket clubs merged to form Ipswich CC.

Clarke, who was previously groundsman at Tattingstone, Woolverstone Park and Copdock, was the driving force behind the creation of the newly-formed club's ground at Clay Hall, which just four years earlier was a field full of stones.

After receiving the award the 61-year-old said: "Originally the club was just going to have one ground, but the opportunity arose to have two and I am now looking at creating a third ground."

Ipswich CC chairman Graham Denny, who nominated Clarke for the award, responded: "He has got it all mapped out how he would like the ground to look in the future, and it is slowly taking shape bit by bit, but sometimes he wants to run before he can walk and we have to keep the reins on him! He has an unending appetite for work.

"He always wanted to create his own cricket ground in his back garden, but this is the nearest he will get to that."

However, the project never got off the ground before Clarke retired in 2014, after serving the club for ten years.

35. Managing expectations

BURY Town boss Richard Wilkins did not hold back.

"I believe Twitter is a poisoned tool for the media. It seems to me it causes more harm than good, as does Facebook," he said.

"From a journalist's point of view it is a heaven, but players don't realise what they put on there sometimes doesn't come across very well." And to think I had only phoned the Bury Town boss in June 2012 to ask about potential comings and goings at the Ryman League Premier Division club ahead of the following season!

In fairness I had seen comments posted on Twitter by some members of his first-team squad, but when I dropped it into our conversation it was like lighting the blue touchpaper with Wilkins.

He continued: "I don't think it is the right thing to do to start plastering details on there which should be between the player and the club.

"It's all right to write on there that you have bought a new pair of shoes, but when you start writing about contractual issues that doesn't seem right to me. You should deal with people face-to-face."

I couldn't have agreed more with Wilkins, but I had landed what ran as a back-page story under the headline 'A poisoned tool' in the following day's *EADT*.

It was in the same month that Wilkins appointed former Luton Town and Cambridge United defender Ben Chenery as his assistant.

Ipswich-based Chenery was available after appearing to carry the can for Chelmsford City failing to win promotion from Blue Square South.

The 35-year-old was number two to former Ipswich Town midfielder Glenn Pennyfather for three seasons, but had just been released after the Clarets lost in the play-offs at the end of the previous season.

Chenery said: "I was very disappointed with the way it was done. I felt it was not justified as I had done a good job, but things change in football and people want to go in a different direction.

"At the time it was very hard to take, and in some ways I felt I was the scapegoat."

Chenery succeeded Wilkins, who stood down after 14 years as Bury Town boss, two years later, but was powerless to prevent Bury from losing their Ryman League Premier Division status at the end of the 2014–15 season.

Another manager to have a rant was Needham Market's Danny Laws, who was left lamenting his side's awful home form.

Laws, who had led his side to the play-offs in each of the previous two seasons, let rip after his side's 3–2 loss at home to Soham Town Rangers in Ryman League Division One North in January 2013.

His frustration boiled over after seeing Needham, who were trailing 2–0 at the interval, equalise, only for substitute Duane Wright to be sent off before the visitors then scored the winner.

The result meant that Needham had failed to win in ten attempts at Bloomfields, and Laws had resigned himself to the fact that promotion was now beyond his side.

He said: "When you look at the table and the column shows no wins at home it is unacceptable and embarrassing for everyone concerned.

"Regardless of our record we cannot perform like that in front of our own supporters and expect any praise whatsoever. Every one of us has a responsibility to put it right."

Laws, who was the subject of my 'Week in the Life' feature on a local non-league manager and what goes on behind-the-scenes a year before, left the club just a month later.

He was replaced by Leiston manager Mark Morsley and ended up heading in the opposite direction to be boss at Leiston instead.

Morsley was not everyone's cup of tea but he was someone who I always got along well with, and he was never short of a quote or two.

He was often happy to tell me information off the record that may be useful at a later date, and he was always a very open and honest person to deal with.

Not many managers would admit to their failings in public, but Morsley did after revamping his Leiston squad following their promotion to the Ryman League Premier Division.

Seven players left Leiston in the summer of 2012 after winning the Division One North title, and several new faces arrived at Victory Road.

But in December of that year, although not naming names, Morsley said: "I didn't know what to expect because I had not experienced this level before, although I always knew it would be tough.

"I think maybe some of the changes in personnel in the summer were mistakes, but that's life. But I made a determined effort to change the way we were playing."

He continued: "There have been games when we have not been good enough, but you learn from those experiences, and I fully believe in the changes we have made, in the way we play, to be right."

Laws, Morsley and Wilkins were all very experienced managers who I dealt with on a regular basis, unlike Hadleigh United's Stuart Crawford.

He had been a player at Hadleigh and was one of the youngest managers in the Ridgeons League when he was appointed at the age of 29 in May 2010.

Crawford, who had not played since snapping the cruciate ligament in his left knee which prematurely ended his career, was facing an injury and unavailability crisis.

Such was his lack of available players he even considered coming out of retirement ahead of the FA Vase third round proper tie at home to Oxhey Jets in December 2012.

Crawford said: "At one stage I even considered getting my boots on as we were so short of players. I was ringing round and waking people up on Saturday morning to see if they could play."

Such was Crawford's predicament that Sam Banya, who had not played for six months and was due to have a cartilage operation the following week, was named in the starting line-up! And Crawford revealed the lengths the club went to so that Jerrell Layne, who had only made his debut for Hadleigh four days earlier, could get to the ground.

He explained: "Jerrell was working in Ipswich on Saturday and didn't finish until 3.30pm. We asked a taxi company if they could pick him up, but they were not keen on doing so as they were concerned who would pay the bill at our end.

"So we sent Kris Rose (Hadleigh's injured defender) to pick him up and he got him back to the ground and changed so that he could come on five minutes into the second half for Sam!"

It was all worth it as Hadleigh won the tie 2–0 and went on to reach the quarter-finals of the competition.

If Crawford, who subsequently led Hadleigh to their first-ever Premier Division title in 2013–14 was a relatively inexperienced manager, Chris Symes was the complete opposite.

Symes, whose remarkable career in football spanned more than 40 years, had coached Scottish First Division side Arbroath, before returning to his home town of Colchester.

He subsequently coached and managed the Essex Senior men's team, Halstead Town, Tiptree United, Braintree Town, Chelmsford City, Brantham Athletic, Bury Town and Wivenhoe Town, before becoming the owner of Cornard United.

When Symes took over the club in 1994 the club's debts totalled £48,000, and he proudly told me that he had reduced the deficit to just £2,200, when I did a feature on his career in January 2009.

Symes devoted countless hours each week to Cornard's cause in a variety of roles. His job description included first-team manager, secretary to four teams that used the ground, groundsman, barman, cleaner, decorator and even disc jockey!

The 63-year-old told me: "Sometimes I think I am mad. My wife says to me 'you haven't got any friends and you drive all our neighbours away at parties talking about football' but as I try to explain to her, I have got friends at Wisbech, Dartford and even the Isle of Wight.

"Wherever I go football people recognise me and give me a Scotch or a smile – they are my friends. When I get fed up I will pack up. I have been fortunate inasmuch as I have now done 1,500 league games and as long as I enjoy it I will keep going.

"It has cost me £50,000 of my own money and an awful lot of hours work, but if I stay at home I get a list of jobs to do, whereas at least I am the boss at the football club!"

Symes was voted top non-league groundsman in East Anglia and the Midlands in 2006, and was always rightly proud of the fact that Cornard United were rarely forced to call off a match.

The walls inside the clubhouse used to be covered with shirts that he had collected, many of them donated by professional clubs who had trained on the Blackhouse Lane pitch.

Symes took a back seat in May 2013 when he announced Mark Hoskins was to take over as manager, before finally selling the club the following year.

36. Coaches corner

'RICHARD Pybus, he of the rapid delivery and persistent no-ball, was sorely missed through injury.

'Fortunately a physiotherapist was on hand at the players' dinner and he was able to come through that engagement with no ill effects.

'Hopefully, he will be fit and roaring next season.'

Those were the words of Suffolk's Minor Counties captain Mark Bailey, exasperated by the absence of his strike bowler through injury, in his captain's report in the county's 1990 handbook, which I was sub-editing at the time.

Bailey's frustration was that he knew, when fit, Pybus was a potential match-winner at Minor Counties level.

He was one of the fastest bowlers outside of the first-class circuit, and an often frightening prospect to play against for club cricketers when firing on all cylinders.

Chris Grove, who was his skipper at Sudbury, told me: "When Sudbury first joined the Two Counties Championship the club played in Division Two for a season and word soon got round that Richard was quite quick.

"That was in the days before helmets were commonplace and I remember batsmen coming out wearing motor-cycle helmets with visors!"

But while the injury-plagued Pybus never fulfilled his undoubted potential on the field, the Whitley Bay-born bowler has certainly excelled since as a coach.

Most coaches who aspire to the international stage have the words 'former Test cricketer' on their CV, which has made the rise of Pybus all the more astounding.

When I was sports editor of the *EADT* Pybus asked me if he could spend some time with me on work experience as he was keen to find out more about how the media worked. Even then he was keen to absorb as much information as possible.

Ten years on from Bailey's summary of his injury-prone fast bowler, Pybus was assisting Pakistan as a coach at the 1999 World Cup in England.

The former Sudbury and Halstead pace ace, keen to enhance his coaching skills, had spent a couple of English winters at Selbourne College in South Africa.

This led to his landing a post with the Border Cricket Academy in East London, helping to develop young players. Among these was Makhaya Ntini, who was subsequently selected as the first ethnically black player to represent South Africa in 1998 and went on to claim more than 300 Test wickets.

Pybus subsequently took over coaching the Border A side, leading the team to both domestic finals in his first season in charge.

After meeting the Pakistan squad while they were on tour in South Africa the previous year, Pybus was invited to be an assistant coach at the World Cup.

Following the resignation of coach Javed Miandad, Pybus was actually in charge of the squad along with skipper Wasim Akram, until the appointment of Mushtaq Mohammed as the new coach just before the start of the tournament. So what was it like working with a team who were renowned for being arguably the most talented but volatile side in international cricket?

Speaking ahead of the tournament, Pybus said: "They are a lovely bunch of guys and a very happy team. All the guys look after each other. There is a lot of respect for the senior players from the youngsters and everyone in the camp is confident.

"I think we will do pretty well if we can get the momentum going. I think South Africa are favourites based on their record over the past couple of years. They are probably the form horse, but, man-for-man, we are probably the most talented side in the World Cup."

Pybus' optimism proved spot on; Pakistan enjoyed a successful tournament, reaching the final at Lord's, before being bowled out for just 132 and tumbling to an eight-wicket loss to Australia.

Since then Pybus has become the most successful coach in South African first-class cricket, guiding the Titans and Cape Cobras to nine championship titles over six seasons, winning the Supersport Series four-day competition four times.

Pybus, who subsequently returned to coach Pakistan, also had a successful spell as coach of the Bangladesh international side and a short stint at Middlesex, stepping down after just five months for personal reasons, before being announced as the West Indies Cricket Board's new director of cricket in October 2013.

Another ex-Suffolk cricketer who graduated to coaching a first-class county was Andy Brown.

The former left-handed batsman had two spells as a player at Derbyshire, before captaining and coaching the county's Second XI.

He then played for and coached Suffolk during one of the most successful periods in the county's history, before agreeing to return to Derbyshire as assistant first-team coach.

Sitting in the Chelmsford sun watching Derbyshire face Essex in the opening match of the 2009 season, Brown recalled going to watch the team he would be inheriting.

He said: "I went to watch Derbyshire up at Headingley against Yorkshire in a one-day game – and I found just the basic disciplines weren't there; arriving on time, getting out on the field on time, having the right kit on.

"It was an absolute shambles. If you can't be organised to do that, how can you be organised about your cricket?"

After realising the size of the task he was taking on alongside director of cricket and first-team coach John Morris, the former England batsman, Brown said the culture had to change.

He added: "Twelve months down the line we have got some very mature cricketers in the changing-room, whereas this time last year I think me and John looked at each other and thought, crikey this is going to be a long slog."

Brown worked in tandem with Kevin Brooks, Suffolk's director of cricket, during his spell with the Minor County.

Brooks was also a former Derbyshire player, before moving to Suffolk to manage a new indoor cricket centre in Ipswich.

I was the first person he met when he arrived in the town in 1985, interviewing him for a feature on the new version of eight-a-side indoor cricket that was played inside a net.

It was to be the start of a friendship that has lasted throughout the intervening three decades.

First through the indoor cricket centre and then through Suffolk, I interviewed Brooks more times than any other individual.

He gave me several 'exclusive' stories such as the signings of Kim Barnett and Neil Foster for the Ipswich indoor cricket team, and then Billy Athey and Hassan Adnan as Suffolk's professionals, Paul Jarvis as coach and engaging international stars as overseas players to appear for Suffolk in the Cheltenham & Gloucester Trophy.

He also set up interviews for me with former international skippers Mike Gatting (England) and David Houghton (Zimbabwe) and even paired me up with Barnett as my room-mate on an away trip while the ex-Derbyshire skipper was playing indoor cricket for Ipswich.

Undoubtedly the biggest coup he pulled off was getting ex-England pace ace Devon Malcolm to sign for Suffolk in 2004.

Malcolm told me: "Kevin contacted me last year and said 'Do you fancy playing for Suffolk?' and I replied 'absolutely no chance' as I had only just retired and wasn't sure what I wanted to do.

"I told him to call me again in the New Year and I would see how my fitness and training programme was going and if I felt like playing. I feel fine and I want to keep playing, so playing in six three-day games as opposed to almost every day of the season won't be a problem for me. I still love the game and have lots of enthusiasm."

Malcolm played nine matches during his two seasons with Suffolk, capturing 34 wickets at 26.55 apiece but also making many friends along the way.

Another story that created a stir was after a video of six-year-old Charlie Allison was posted on the Internet in January 2012.

The video was shot by his coach Ben Stephens, an opening bowler who played for Colchester & East Essex and the previous season had represented Suffolk in the Minor Counties KO Trophy.

The clip on YouTube showcased Charlie batting in the nets reeling off his favourite shots – cover drives, pulls, hooks and even reverse sweeps – while displaying a technique way beyond his tender years.

The video was viewed more than 118,000 times in the first month after it was posted, and news of his batting prowess spread like wildfire.

He was featured on Sky TV and in national newspapers and the story was even picked up by Indian TV, with Charlie being dubbed 'six-year-old Sachin' after Indian superstar batsman Sachin Tendulkar.

To get a different angle on the story I spoke to Stephens, who had set up cricket bat and equipment manufacturing company PiriPiri Cricket with Steve Parnell a couple of years earlier.

He said that Charlie, the youngest of three brothers, came to his attention when his dad Tom went to sign him up for a winter course he was running for under-11s.

At first he said no, but Tom convinced him Charlie would be alright as he was used to playing against his older brothers, so he agreed Charlie could attend the first session.

Stephens, who was just 25 at the time, said that when it came to

Charlie's turn to bat he had 11-year-olds bowling to him, so he told him to take his time as the ball would be coming at him quicker than he was used to and to try to get in line and not to try any attacking shots.

"The first ball he faced he took a couple of steps down the wicket and played a good defensive shot. He then left the next ball, which was outside off stump and swung, and the next ball was a half volley outside off stump and he reverse swept it!

"I stood there in amazement. I said to Charlie 'I said no attacking shots' and he replied 'It was along the ground' and my chin just dropped," recalled Stephens.

He said that PiriPiri ran a sponsorship scheme for talented young cricketers and as he had agreed to sponsor both Ben and Ollie, Charlie's older brothers, all three visited his shop along with their dad to buy some gear.

"Charlie picked up the smallest bat he could find and I said he could have it on condition I made a video, which we did.

"I had never made a video before and I shot it on my iphone and then edited it before putting it live on the Internet at 10 o'clock on the Saturday night.

"I tweeted it to a couple of celebrities and within the hour (ex-Essex captain) Ronnie Irani had retweeted it. When I checked at 11.30pm it had already received 450 hits, and it just took off from there. By the time I went to bed on the Monday night 12,000 viewers had watched it.

"That night my phone started going nuts and around midnight I found Cricket Australia had tweeted it. The number of hits went from 12,000 to 42,000 in just six hours."

37. Executive decisions

SUFFOLK FA was still being run by an honorary county secretary from his own home up until around the turn of the new Millennium.

That was a far cry from a decade later when the county had a chief executive, nine other full-time staff and four part-time staff working out of the county's own headquarters at Stowmarket.

The man heading up the operation was Martin Head, who was county secretary before becoming the first chief executive of Suffolk FA.

It was in that role that his job was to oversee the transformation of how football was run in the county.

So when I took Suffolk FA to task over the timing of their cup draws in October 2009, I was delighted when Head told me they had taken on board what I had said.

I criticised Suffolk FA in my 'Scene & Heard' blog on the *Green 'Un* website for being 'killjoys' in staging the draws for the quarter-finals of the 2009–10 season before the majority of the first-round ties had even taken place.

All bar one tie – that involving Debenham LC and Bury Town – which had been played the previous week, were scheduled for that week and yet the draw had been held live on Radio Suffolk at tea-time the previous Saturday.

My point was that clubs knew who they would be facing in the next round, before even kicking a ball, which I didn't feel was right, and that some clubs may approach their first-round ties differently knowing who their opponents in the last eight would be.

So when Head contacted me to say that the county competitions committee had considered my comments and taken note, I felt it was a victory for common sense.

He said that Suffolk FA sympathised with my point of view and that they would try to ensure ties were not pre-drawn in the future – a point I am pleased to say has been adhered to ever since.

Head stepped down after eight years in charge soon after overseeing Suffolk's 125th anniversary celebrations in December 2010.

Two years later it was the turn of Essex County Cricket Club chief executive David East to say his goodbyes following a 30-year association with the club.

East joined Essex in 1981 as a wicket-keeper/batsman and was part of a highly successful era that saw Essex capture three county championship titles.

Seven years after his first-class career was ended through injury, East returned to the County Ground at Chelmsford as commercial manager in 1998, before being appointed as chief executive two years later.

I went so far as to tip East to be successor to Peter Edwards, the club's long-serving secretary/general manager who died of a heart attack while on a winter tour to South Africa in January 2000, in the article I wrote following his death.

We had always enjoyed a good rapport and at least once a season, sometimes at the annual Press Day and on other occasions during the course of the season, used to catch up and discuss key issues.

I remembered he was particularly excited about one topic he told me about in March 2002.

He said: "I believe in county cricket at the moment that we are very product driven but need to move towards being more market driven.

"Unless we provide a product at the right price and at a time when spectators can come and watch then it could spell disaster."

Guessed it? East was backing plans to introduce a new competition the following season which was seen as a replacement to the Benson & Hedges Cup, otherwise now known as Twenty20 cricket.

On his departure from Essex a decade later, East told me: "Twenty20 cricket has been the most radical change with the revenue it has brought in.

"At Essex we identified a market for Twenty20 cricket and have maximised revenue from it. Hopefully this will continue in the future."

Another man with vision was David Folb, the businessman, entrepreneur and founder of the Lashings World XI cricket team.

It was back in 1984 that Folb was in the Lashings Bar and Restaurant in Maidstone on a Saturday night when he heard that the nearby Minstrel's Wine Bar cricket team had been let down by their scheduled opponents the following day.

Folb made a few phone calls and assembled a team to play the following day. Although they were soundly beaten by 294 runs, Folb's team had caught the bug and soon regular matches were taking place.

It was in 1995 when Folb was visiting Antigua, where he had opened the Lashings Beach Café Inn, that he met West Indian skipper Richie Richardson, who was about to retire from international cricket.

He was seeking a fun, no-pressure environment to play in and rediscover his love of the game, and agreed to sign for Folb's team.

However, this was laughed off by the local media who did not believe such a high-profile cricketer as Richardson was coming to play for a village side in Kent.

I interviewed Folb at Haverhill Cricket Club towards the end of the season in 2009, when I asked him did he really envisage his pub side would grow into the global brand it had become?

He said: "I am a pretty positive sort of person and I think that the people who played against Lashings when we were a pub/village team would always tell you I had big ambitions for the club, so the answer is yes, I did.

"That might sound arrogant, but I did. I have always shot for the top and then seen where we have got to. Yes, I was pretty confident that we would grow into a big club at one stage."

Many of the world's top former players – plus quite a few current international stars – have since donned the famous yellow and black Lashings kit to play for Folb's all-star team.

They have become a cricketing equivalent of the Harlem Globetrotters, raising thousands of pounds in the process.

The man who had been charged with running the day-to-day operation in his role as Lashings' chief executive at that time was Andrew Fitch-Holland.

After meeting him at a benefit dinner for Nick Knight at Felsted School, where the former England batsman was once a pupil, I arranged to interview Fitch-Holland. He was a trained lawyer who worked for the Crown Prosecution Service, before taking a career break to spend more time with his family.

He landed the Lashings post after impressing Folb with his organising and fundraising skills and drive and enthusiasm – and was clearly relishing his role when we spoke.

He said: "We have an almost evangelical zeal for growing the game. We will go anywhere to play anyone in an attempt to broaden the game's horizons.

"We played on a beach in Scotland at low tide and two days later were playing the Scottish national team in Edinburgh in front of thousands."

The prospect of the likes of Sir Viv Richards, Brian Lara, Mark Waugh, Allan Donald and Wasim Akram coming to play at your local club or school was one without comparison.

Fitch-Holland said: "It is one of the most extraordinary stories in sport. The only way I can describe it is if Pele, Sir Bobby Charlton, Thierry Henry and David Beckham turned up to play in your local park for a kick around."

After seeing several matches involving Lashings and meeting Fitch-Holland, I saw a potential opportunity and he agreed to meet with me to discuss my idea.

It was the following spring when we met at the waterside pub The Swan in Great Henny, just outside Sudbury.

Fitch-Holland was accompanied by his two daughters, but we got down to talking about my proposal which revolved around Lashings employing me as a media officer.

I envisaged this would involve producing a yearbook with player profiles, publicising Lashings matches with previews and reports, producing player interviews, plus handling media enquiries.

It was during the course of our conversation that Fitch-Holland's mobile rang and he duly answered it.

He came off the phone to tell me that we were about to be joined for lunch by Geoff Miller, who was on his way over after visiting the county Ground at Chelmsford.

My job pitch was about to be hijacked by England's national cricket selector!

Sadly for me, Fitch-Holland never did take me up on my offer.

It was several years later that I finally visited the Lashings bar and restaurant in Maidstone.

A wry smile passed across my face as we sat down at our table to be greeted with, you've guessed it, a Lashings Yearbook...

Part Nine
– Sporting potpourri

38. Colourful characters

HE played first-class cricket for Nottinghamshire and Essex, trialled as a pitcher for six Major League USA baseball teams and also pioneered the introduction of coloured cricket clothing in this country.

That was before he started his own fast bowling workshops, leading to work with Kent and Warwickshire, and then became bowling coach to Essex, Northamptonshire and the Dutch national side.

Since then he has worked with leading international bowlers including the world-ranked number one Dale Steyn, and had a successful stint as Bangladesh's bowling coach, the team winning 11 of 14 one-day internationals during his time in charge.

His CV includes spells as a coach at three Cricket World Cups and back-to-back Bangladesh Premier League titles as head coach of the Dhaka Gladiators. On top of that he has also written three books and even presented his own radio show on BBC Essex.

He still plays a decent standard of cricket, including turning out for the successful Essex Over-50s side, coaches all over the world and has spent the past five years mentoring Catherine Dalton, one of the rising stars of the English women's game.

There is no doubt that Ian Pont is the most colourful character I have come across in my career as a sports journalist – and Essex County Cricket Club have certainly had more than their fair share over the years.

Pont is a fascinating person to talk to, not only has he got a stack of stories in common with most ex-professional sportsmen but his rich and varied past make him stand out from the crowd.

His own coaching company is called Mavericks Cricket Institute, and when I interviewed him for my 'Love Cricket' Column in the *EADT* and *Evening Star* in the summer of 2010, he admitted: "I chose the Mavericks name as I wanted to be different and for people to remember the name."

We met at a hotel between Colchester and Pont's home in Halstead, and the interview turned into the longest one I have ever done – it was a full two-and-a-half hours before we finally called time and said our goodbyes.

Typical of Pont, talking about the 2007 World Cup in the West Indies for which he had helped the Netherlands to qualify, was the quip: "I remember sitting at breakfast with the likes of Ricky Ponting and Greg Chappell and I am thinking to myself I am the only person I have never heard of at the table!"

One of Pont's team-mates in the Essex Over-50s side that reached the national final in 2014, before losing to Durham by just six runs, was ex-Essex batsman Chris Gladwin.

The left-hander was at one stage Graham Gooch's opening partner at Essex and considered a potential future England player.

But he never realised his potential, playing just 71 first-class matches, latterly for Derbyshire, between 1981 and 1989.

At the start of the 1988 season Gladwin joined Minor Counties side Suffolk, who already had several colourful characters in their ranks, notably Phil Caley, Simon Clements, Justin Edrich and Gordon Morgan.

Gladwin could dismantle any attack in double-quick time, but all too often his innings were cameos as he failed to go on and get a big score. That was not the case when he struck 171 off just 116 deliveries in an unbroken stand of 295 with another ex-Essex batsman Mike McEvoy (113 not out) as Suffolk defeated Northumberland by ten wickets at Jesmond in May 1990. The partnership still stands as the record for the county's first-wicket.

Gladwin could also bowl medium-pace and spin and was a superb catcher. He also had a penchant for magic tricks.

I will never forget how he had everyone around the bar after a day's play against Durham at Hartlepool spellbound.

Gladwin could drop a pint mug on to his foot without spilling it, stub a cigarette butt out in a jumper but not leave a burn mark and stick a knife through a ten pound note with no visible sign of a cut. The Durham boys absolutely lapped it up.

Former Essex slow left armer Ray East was well-known for his antics on the field, and also an entertainer off it. East, one of the most naturally funny guys I have met, was invited to speak at my cricket club Copdock's 150th anniversary dinner at the Moat House, opposite the ground just outside Ipswich, in the summer of 1989.

He was appearing alongside Christopher Martin-Jenkins, the BBC cricket correspondent and *Daily Telegraph* cricket journalist.

It was the first time I had heard East speak, and to this day I stand by what I said then that anyone walking into the room who did not know any different would not have been able to tell who was getting paid £500 and who was getting a bottle of whisky for their efforts.

That is in no way disrespectful to CMJ, but a measure of just how good East was on the after-dinner circuit.

Around that time East and his then wife Barbara ran the Red Lion at East Bergholt, and as by then he was turning out for the village side and there was no bar at the club's Gandish Road ground, it was back to the pub after the game.

There were some lively characters that played for East Bergholt in those days, not least David Goodchild, Archie Lea, Chris and Dennis McGrath and Robert Shurety, and evenings at the Red Lion often turned into memorable occasions.

It was not unusual for almost the entire bar to end up standing on tables and chairs, some banging trays against their heads, singing *Sunshine Mountain* at the tops of their voices.

As with a lot of extrovert characters, East had a different side to him as I once found to my cost!

East skippered Suffolk during the 1992 and 1993 seasons. A successful first summer saw Suffolk qualify for the following year's NatWest Trophy and a home match against his former county Essex at Bury St Edmunds.

However, the second season proved more challenging for East and he took umbrage at what I wrote in my end-of-season review in the *EADT* and *Evening Star* under the headline: 'Pride lost as Suffolk finish in a shambles.'

I wrote: 'His pledge when he took over the captaincy that he wanted to put the pride back into Suffolk cricket had a rather hollow ring in the second half of the campaign.

'East himself failed to take a single wicket in the 65 overs he sent down and the strain of his second season in charge at the age of 46 took its toll.'

Fair comment, or so I thought, considering Suffolk finished bottom of the ten-team table with just 43 points accrued from nine matches.

It was at the Two Counties cricket dinner, where East was the guest speaker, that he took me to task soon after.

Three times East referred to me as 'Poison Pen' Garnham during his speech – I think I got more mentions than the sponsors – as he left me in no uncertain terms as to what he thought of the article.

Suffice to say that no more was ever said thereafter and East has always since been very welcoming and accommodating when I have been in his company.

Another extrovert character, who played for Essex, was Mark Ilott.

The left-arm pace bowler, who played five Tests for England, was nicknamed 'Ramble' during a 15-year career. And if you've ever met him, you'll know why!

Ilott once told me that he was a 'people's person – I love organising things' as he spent part of the winter of 1999–2000 in his role as secretary of the Essex County Cricket Benefit Association, which runs during those years when no player is awarded a benefit.

That was in-between two days a week in the City working in PR and his appearances for the likes of Sky TV as an analyst.

"I am busier in the winter months than I am in the summer," he said tongue firmly in cheek as we chatted about England's prospects during that winter's tour of South Africa.

I once rang Ilott the day before a one-day cup game in his hotel room to do a preview piece. All was going well until he just went completely off the subject and literally rambled on about nothing in particular. Cue end of interview!

Stuart Law, who spent seven seasons at Essex until his acrimonious departure in 1992, was the complete opposite of Ilott – a typical straight-talking Australian.

So I was surprised when he became a British citizen, and tackled him on the subject soon after he had qualified when we spoke at Culford School, where he was appearing for the Lashings All-Star XI, just ahead of the 2009 Ashes Series. A smile broke out over his face as soon as I brought the topic up in conversation and he laughed in anticipation of the inevitable question – where did his loyalties lie?

"I am a very loyal person – Australia to win 3–1," was his no-nonsense reply.

Law, who played for Lancashire until 2008 and then signed a one-day contract with Derbyshire the following summer, remained a big fan of English cricket, although not the volume of matches.

"The amount of cricket we play still kills it. It could be a hell of a lot better, but unfortunately for the players no one seems to take any notice of them!

"We keep saying we are playing too much cricket and they throw in another competition which makes it tough on the body," he stated.

Law, who led Queensland to the domestic Sheffield Shield title Down Under, added: "In county cricket you might have finished on a Sunday after playing five days in a row, and after a day off you are starting again. When that Tuesday comes round you don't really want to get out of bed!"

It was during the summer of 2009 while with Derbyshire that Law showcased the Mongoose cricket bat, described as the most radical change to equipment since 1771.

The Mongoose – a smaller blade with a longer handle which claimed to give batsmen more bat speed than conventional bats – was specifically designed for T20 and Law believed it had the potential to revolutionise cricket.

He told me: "It is exciting to be involved in something that is so different. I have used it and I believe in it which is why I have put my name to it."

Despite Law's enthusiasm for the Mongoose, it has never really caught on in this country and is still on the loose.

Geoff Miller, who went on to become England's National Selector, summed up the changing landscape of characters in sport in this country.

Miller spent three memorable seasons at Essex, who he joined in 1987, between two stints at Derbyshire.

The former England all-rounder, who was speaking at a Sporting Dinner in Ipswich in May 2002, told me: "There was a great camaraderie in the dressing room.

"It took them a year or so to understand my northern accent and humour, but there were some great characters in the side like Ray East, John Lever, Brian Hardie and Alan Lilley."

Miller, who appeared in 34 Tests and 25 one-day internationals, added: "The game has altered a lot since then. The characters were allowed to shine through.

"The game today is much more professional. There are still

characters, but the priorities have altered. There is more emphasis placed on the results today, so the characters don't get so much opportunity."

39. Stalwarts and veterans

JOHN Stuck thought he would be a club scorer rather than still scoring centuries at the age of 65.

There was not any veterans' cricket played in his younger days, and Stuck envisaged he would turn his hand to being a club scorer in his later years. But the former Suffolk batsman racked up the 150th century of his career in the summer of 2009 after scoring hundreds on successive days.

No mean feat for a batsman who once turned down a five-year scholarship at Lord's to try and make it as a first-class cricketer because he didn't think he was good enough.

After reaching the milestone Stuck told me: "I still love batting, and batting a long time, but I have always been a team member, and anyone who calls me a selfish batsman has got the wrong idea."

Stuck had already passed 1,000 runs for the season to take his career aggregate soaring beyond a staggering 90,000, a large percentage of which he made for club side Clacton.

He said he was only aware of one other batsman then still playing – Andy Meads of Sussex side Three Bridges – to have scored 150 centuries in club cricket.

Stuck, who the previous year was named joint Man of the Match in the inaugural Over-60s Test between England and Australia held near Melbourne, said modestly: "Mine have come over a long period of time. I don't think it is a huge achievement.

"I think the achievement is being able to play so much over that period of time in order to be able to do that."

Tony Warrington hung up his bat at the age of 60 in the summer of 2008, after a career spanning 46 run-laden seasons.

Warrington, like Stuck, opened the batting for Suffolk and was the county's all-time highest individual run-scorer.

He scored 111 centuries during an illustrious career, starring for Ipswich side Browns and Bury St Edmunds, but revealed he started out as an opening bowler!

Following his retirement Warrington said: "I bowled away swing at school and batted at No.3, but when I started playing men's cricket at the age of 14 I didn't get the chance to bowl and lost it.

"It was the late Ted Cunnell (father to former Suffolk skipper Bob and his brother Cliff) who made me into an opening batsman. Thereafter I bowled a bit of off spin and a bit of filfth out of the back of the hand!"

Warrington played in 14 different countries and at more than 400 grounds over the course of his career, during which he was selected for both the Minor Counties and NCA (England Amateur XI) representative sides and also regularly represented the MCC.

It was a case of have boots, will travel for Martin Southwell, who enjoyed racking up centuries of a different kind.

When I interviewed Southwell in the summer of 2011 he was on course to complete a century of appearances for the third year in a row.

A cricketing nomad if ever there was one, Southwell had appeared for an incredible 17 different sides during that time!

Southwell, who lived in Heybridge Basin, admitted: "If the truth were known, it could be said that I am a bit of a cricket tart, and anybody's for a game of cricket and a slice of cake!"

The 59-year-old all-rounder revealed the secret behind his ability to play so many matches each season.

"Well, I guess it's because I keep reasonably fit by lots of walking and swimming most days, playing a bit of hockey and squash, and also by protecting damaged and broken fingers with bubble wrap instead of being sensible and waiting for injuries to heal. It also helps to be single."

Goalkeeper Andy Mustoe, in complete contrast, was awarded a testimonial match by West Suffolk village side Stanton, after making more than 650 appearances for the club.

The club marked Mustoe's milestone in May 2012 with a match between past and present players.

On the eve of the match the 40-year-old revealed: "I tried to join Stanton when I was 17, but I was told I was too young, so I played a handful of games for Sicklesmere, before signing for the 1990–91 season."

Mustoe went on to skipper Stanton for eight seasons, and one of the highlights of his career came in 2001–02 when he lined-up against his twin brother Doug, who at the time played in goal for Walsham-le-Willows, in the Omnico Cup Final.

Paul Betson racked up 376 appearances – more than any other player – for Suffolk's leading non-league side AFC Sudbury, after signing for the club at the start of the 1999–00 season.

The left-sided player appeared in all three of the club's FA Vase Finals in successive seasons between 2003 and 2005 – all of which ended in defeat.

He topped a list of Sudbury's all-time leading appearance makers that included such stalwarts as Andrew 'Porky' Claydon, Chris Tracey, David Head, Terry Rayner, Lee Owen, Lee Norfolk, Simon Hyde, Brett Girling, Gary Bennett and Shane Wardley.

Betson, who moved to Ipswich Wanderers in December 2006, told me: "I am very proud of that.

"That was a special time in my career and also for the club. There was always something happening – we were either involved in big cup matches or challenging for the league, so every game was important."

Betson, who also played for Braintree Town, Felixstowe & Walton

United and Lakenheath, was still going strong approaching his 38th birthday when I interviewed him.

By then he was with Newmarket Town, who he had just helped to win promotion back to the Thurlow Nunn Premier Division at the first attempt.

Despite his advancing years Betson had clearly lost none of his appetite for the game.

"I still love it – I really do. I love it as much now as I have always done," he said.

Another stalwart I interviewed was Paul Musgrove, who had just clocked up his 350th appearance for Thurlow Nunn League Premier Division side Walsham-le-Willows.

Musgrove had to overcome a double blow as a teenager, before embarking on his successful non-league career.

After training with Ipswich Town from the age of nine, Musgrove was released by the club as a 16-year-old, and inside three weeks suffered an even more crushing blow when his mum, Diane, died from cancer.

The 31-year-old admitted: "It knocked my confidence at the time, but it made me stronger."

Musgrove, who subsequently had trials with both Colchester United and Lincoln City, failed to carve out a career as a professional footballer.

But after a short spell at Bury Town the then 17-year-old joined Walsham, who at the time were still a Senior Division side in the Suffolk & Ipswich League.

And apart from brief spells at Mildenhall Town and Needham Market, Musgrove remained loyal to Walsham thereafter.

Former Ipswich Town midfielder Gavin Johnson was a team-mate of Musgrove's during the twilight of both their careers.

Johnson, who scored Ipswich Town's first-ever goal in the new FA Premier League – on the opening day of the 1992–93 season at home to Aston Villa – continued to play at non-league level after he had finished as a professional.

And that was despite suffering cruciate injuries to both knees and breaking the same leg twice earlier in his career!

Johnson, who also played for Bury Town and Needham Market before returning to Old Newton United, said he was grateful to the surgeon who operated on his broken leg for extending his career.

The surgeon questioned how long Johnson intended to continue playing, before deciding what to do.

Johnson, who at the time was playing for Needham Market when we spoke in March 2012, said: "I told him I wished to carry on for a few years, so he decided to put a plate and screws in, and it proved to be a great decision as it has enabled me to continue my career."

The 41-year-old, whose Football League clubs also included Colchester United, Luton Town and Wigan Athletic, suffered cruciate injuries to both knees while with Ipswich Town between 1989 and 1995.

He continued: "I injured both knees more than 20 years ago. I was lucky that David Dandy, who was based in Cambridge, was one of the top surgeons in the world, and he successfully operated on both of them.

"It was not long before, that if a player suffered a cruciate injury, they had to retire."

40. Three Wise Men

NORMAN Smith simply *had* to go to the Cup Final.

After all he had done for Suffolk Schools' football, it would be a travesty if he was not at Hillsborough.

But there was one major obstacle stopping him from attending – and that was Smith himself.

Although a sprightly 93-year-old he was refusing to travel to the English Schools' Football Association Under-16 Inter-County Trophy for Boys' Cup Fnal because he didn't want to be a burden to anyone.

The problem was that the Suffolk squad were travelling up the afternoon before the match in May 2010, and Smith did not want to be out of his 'comfort zone' by staying in an hotel overnight.

So I hatched a plan to ensure that Smith, who had been a stalwart servant of Suffolk County Schools' Football Association for more than half a century, would be present.

It involved me driving to his home in Woodbridge and picking him up and taking him to Bury St Edmunds, where we would meet up with Andy Abbott, the chief photographer at Archant Suffolk.

Abbott would then drive us both to Sheffield, which would enable me to not only keep Smith company in the back of the car but also to interview him.

An in-depth interview on Smith's association with schools' football in Suffolk was long overdue, and my plan ensured there was no way he would be able to escape my clutches.

Smith, a former school teacher, had always been a stickler for detail who was never afraid to call up the newspaper's offices to point out that the word 'schools' had been omitted from the title 'Suffolk County Schools' FA' or to voice his disapproval at the use of the word 'clash' to describe two teams playing each other.

His memory was still razor-sharp, and he was much easier to extract information from than subjects even a third of his age.

Detail about his personal background and association with Suffolk County Schools' FA tripped off his tongue, but what I was most keen to hear was which one player to represent the county had stood out above all others?

Although he had seen a whole host of youngsters who had gone on to not only play professionally but also represent their country, Smith didn't hesitate to answer.

"Jason Dozzell," he replied instantly. "There are many others I could think of but his name came immediately to me.

"The way he moved was effortless. Other people were good, but he was a natural player in the way he moved.

"I saw him score on his debut for Ipswich Town at Portman Road and was very proud."

Indeed, Dozzell still holds the record as the youngest goalscorer in the top flight of English football aged 16 years and 57 days, after coming on as a substitute against Coventry City on 4 February 1984.

Smith also recalled the most memorable moments of the previous 55 years, which involved Suffolk Schools' FA reaching Cup Finals on four separate occasions.

Suffolk had won the previous three, but there was to be no victory celebrations later in the day as Suffolk lost 5–1 to Greater Manchester, but at least Smith was there to witness it.

The manner in which he described the way Dozzell moved reminded me of my meeting with John Elsworthy some two-and-a-half years earlier.

Elsworthy was a member of the Ipswich Town team that were the last opposition to face Manchester United at Old Trafford before the Munich Air Disaster on 6 February, 1958.

The crash claimed the lives of eight of the 'Busby Babes' including five who had featured in that FA Cup fourth-round tie just 12 days earlier.

Ahead of the 50th anniversary of the tragedy that rocked world football, I had arranged to interview Elsworthy at his Ipswich home.

Even half a century on Elsworthy still struggled to make sense of the loss of life.

Elsworthy and his Ipswich team-mates gave a good account of themselves in front of 53,550 – the biggest crowd to ever watch an Ipswich match at the time – despite losing 2–0.

Twelve days later five of that United side – Roger Byrne, Eddie Colman, Mark Jones, Duncan Edwards and Tommy Taylor – lost their lives. They were among the 23 of 44 passengers who died as the plane carrying the United team, club officials and journalists, crashed on take-off at Munich in West Germany, as they returned from playing Yugoslavian side Red Star Belgrade in a European Cup tie.

Elsworthy recalled: "We felt dreadful. We were devastated. They were such a lovely bunch of fellas. It just happened so suddenly.

"The players at Ipswich could not believe it. Players went around in a trance. Having only just played against them, some of the players took it very badly."

Both United goals against Ipswich were scored by Bobby Charlton, and it was mention of his name that sparked the comparison of my subsequent interview with Norman Smith.

Although aged 76, Elsworthy still looked fit and he showed it by getting up out of his chair to demonstrate what made the young Charlton such a special player even then.

Moving sideways across the room of his home to illustrate his point as he spoke with great enthusiasm, Elsworthy recalled: "In my day you had to be good over two yards.

"He (Charlton) would make room for himself and be gone. He had electrifying pace and you could not do anything about it."

The two hours that I spent at the Elwsorthy household on a dank Friday afternoon in January 2008 remain among the most magical in my time as a sports journalist.

For although Elsworthy, generally regarded as the best uncapped Welshman of his era, was suffering from Alzheimer's Disease and repeated himself on several occasions, his detailed memory of events half a century before were pure gold.

The same can be said of my interview with former Suffolk cricketer Cyril Perkins ahead of celebrating his 100th birthday.

Perkins, who was the country's oldest living former first-class cricketer, was, and still is, Suffolk's leading all-time record wicket-taker.

The slow left-armer bagged 779 victims at an average of 13.34 with best figures of 10 for 23 against Hertfordshire on 20 August, 1960 – the only Suffolk player to ever claim all ten wickets in an innings.

His tally of wickets is put firmly into context by the fact that the next highest on the county's all-time wicket-taking list is Colin Rutterford with a mere 431!

Knowing that Perkins, who I had never met before, was soon to celebrate his milestone I visited the house where he still lived alone on Bramford Road in Ipswich a month before his birthday.

Although he was sceptical at first about being interviewed he subsequently agreed for me to return along with Archant Suffolk chief photographer Abbott.

My 'groundwork' had paid dividends, as Perkins said he had declined approaches from other media, including Sky Sports, in the meantime for interviews.

Perkins posed for some photographs before he recalled how he nearly played against Sir Donald Bradman, the greatest cricketer ever to live, when Australia visited England in 1934.

At the time Perkins was on the staff at first-class county

Northamptonshire, who he said in those days, partly to save on expenses, used to bring in amateurs for the match against the tourists.

"We brought in two amateurs, and I was one of those who had to stand down and make way!

"I was the duty telephone boy and spent the match at the top of the pavilion. I don't actually recall Bradman batting, but he was bowled by my old school friend, Reg Partridge, I think for a duck."

Perkins, who played against the likes of Harold Larwood, Hedley Verity, Herbert Sutcliffe and Maurice Leyland, also talked about how the game has evolved over the years.

"The biggest difference is in the fielding. In my day it didn't do to have a grass stain on your flannels! If you could not stop the ball with your foot it usually went all the way to the boundary.

"Now they dive and dash about and it is a wonder they don't hurt themselves. I think it is amazing the way some of them are able to stop the ball in the field."

41. It's just not cricket

THE two black and white photographs hanging on the wall were there to act as an icebreaker to Neil Foster's past life.

On the left was one of Australian batsman Allan Border having one of his stumps knocked out of the ground at Old Trafford.

On the right was one of Foster, flanked by Graham Gooch and Graham Dilley, being introduced to the Queen during a Test match at Lord's.

They illustrated two proud moments in a successful career with Essex and England but one prematurely ended at the age of just 31 after undergoing 13 operations.

One major back operation and three subsequent minor ones, plus no less than nine knee operations had taken their toll.

In the end the pain became too much and Foster packed away his bowling boots back in 1993.

He spent a couple of years teaching PE at Holmwood House Prep School in Colchester, before becoming development coach with Northamptonshire County Cricket Club, running their youth system.

But after moving lock, stock and barrel, Foster's family never rally settled in the county. His wife Lorraine sat him down one day and asked him what he was going to do with the rest of his life.

It was then that Foster decided to train as a physiotherapist.

Foster recalled: "I had always been interested in physiotherapy. Because I had so many operations I started to ask questions about why I was receiving the treatment that I was undergoing.

"While I was injured I bought a sport injuries book – not to check up on what I was being told but to gain more knowledge on what I was having done to me."

So ten years after quitting first-class cricket through injury, Foster was treating patients in his physiotherapy and sports injury clinic from the front room of his East Bergholt home.

A month into his new career Foster told me: "I have had a couple of people come in who are keen on their cricket but not realised who I am.

"When we have got chatting they have said 'so you're that Neil Foster' when they have realised what I used to do."

Which is why the two black and white photographs were hanging from the wall behind the couch as a link to his sporting past.

While training part-time to be a physio, Foster had a spell as bowling coach with former county Essex.

And it was during that time that he watched Ashley Cowan on the recommendation of Framlingham College cricket coach Colin Rutterford.

So it was rather ironic that Cowan, like Foster, saw his first-class career end early through injury.

A degenerative knee condition had plagued Cowan for four seasons, before he broke down and had to undergo major surgery on his right knee that saw him sidelined for the entire 2003 season.

The uncertainty surrounding Cowan's future served as a reminder how fickle a professional sportsman's career can be.

The 28-year-old told me: "Up to that point last season I was bowling as well as ever.

"We all knew the injury was going to flare up at some stage as it has been getting progressively worse year by year.

"But I was bowling well, the team were winning, we reached the Final of the Benson & Hedges Cup and I felt perhaps it was my year, but deep down I knew this was an accident waiting to happen."

A trip to Munich to undergo a pioneering technique, which it was hoped would avoid the necessity for major surgery, proved unsuccessful. Cowan was left with two options – either quit playing professional cricket or undergo the operation that could save his career.

He chose the latter; a small sample of his old cartilage was removed and sent to Denmark to be cultured, before the new growth was plugged back into the knee.

After returning to action during the second half of the 2004 season he struggled to make an impact the following year, before announcing his retirement in July 2006. It was a brave attempt to try to resurrect a career that had seen him selected to tour the West Indies with England at the age of just 22, although he never got to play in a Test match.

He reflected: "I hoped to play but didn't get picked. I was fit but Angus Fraser had one of those tours as a bowler when everything went exceptionally well for him.

"Myself and (Yorkshire bowler) Chris Silverwood were waiting for our chance if someone got injured."

Silverwood, ironically, joined the coaching staff at Essex, after his first-class career came to an end.

He was about to be released by Middlesex at the end of the 2009 season when I caught up with him.

He had spent that summer turning out for Haverhill Cricket Club in Division Two of the Marshall Hatchick Two Counties Championship as player-coach when not required by Middlesex.

The 34-year-old got involved at Haverhill after moving to nearby Withersfield with wife Victoria, who worked in the horse racing industry.

The couple kept seven horses in stables at their Suffolk farm, two of which were at the time training with none other than Henry Cecil, widely regarded as one of the greatest trainers in history.

Living on the doorstep of Newmarket, the headquarters of the horse racing industry, had fuelled Silverwood's passion for the Sport of Kings.

While watching his Haverhill team-mates batting at Ipswich CC, Silverwood said: "It is a great getaway from cricket for me going up to Henry's and going to the gallops and having a cup of tea and talking with him about different things.

"It helps me get away from cricket and to put things back into perspective, which sometimes you need. It is a great occupation, but sometimes it does feel like a job, so it is great to get away.

"I find it fascinating as well. It is one of the few sports that I find brings every walk of life together and you are all equal."

Silverwood revealed that when he called time on his first-class career, Cecil had mentioned the possibility of developing his interest further, by spending a couple of months working for him learning the ropes.

"To be honest, my skill is in cricket. It is what I have grown up doing and is what I know and sometimes you are just better off sticking with what you know," he said.

While spending that winter in Zimbabwe as player-coach of Mashonaland Eagles, one of the first-class franchises based in Harare, Silverwood was offered the post of bowling coach at Essex, and any thoughts of a career in the horse racing industry were shelved indefinitely.

Essex wicket-keeper James Foster, like Cowan and Silverwood, knows what it's like to spend time away on tour and be on the fringes of the action.

Foster had already toured Zimbabwe (where he made his one-day international debut), India (scene of his Test debut) and New Zealand when he was picked as understudy to Alec Stewart to tour Australia in 2002–03.

Foster played in the Fourth Test, which England lost by five wickets, but was otherwise left kicking his heels during the series.

So was spending three months in Australia with a group of mates and being paid for it a dream come true or just another job?

Foster told me: "At times it is a bit difficult, but it is part and parcel of the job.

"We very rarely got days off. Our routine was a bit like Ground-hog Day. We normally got up early and trained in the morning and then did some fitness work in the afternoon.

"You would feel pretty tired at the end of the day and have a kip in your room before going out for a bite to eat."

Sleeping in different beds is an occupational hazard for any professional sportsman when on tour or playing away from home.

But it presented more of a problem to Will Jefferson than most during his first-class career, when he was the tallest player on the circuit.

The opening batsman, who started his career at Essex and later had spells at Nottinghamshire and Leicestershire, stood 6ft, 10in tall.

Jefferson, who was touted as a potential future England player early on in his career, slept in a specially made 7ft, 6in long bed in his Chelmsford digs.

Ahead of the 2003 season he told me how he had prevented any particular problems the previous summer when sleeping in smaller hotel beds.

"I would put a chair at the end of the bed and put pillows on top to put my feet on. When we played Leicestershire at Grace Road I did get a double bed and could sleep diagonally!" he explained.

While studying at Durham University he would often have to make long journeys to play for Essex, and sitting in an uncomfortable position in the car damaged his back.

He missed most of the 2001 season after undergoing an operation on a prolapsed disc, before finding the car of his dreams – a Toyota Yaris Verso, which had more headroom than any other car he had come across.

"When I was at Durham I sat in 20 to 25 cars, but I couldn't find one with enough space for me to sit comfortably. In this car I can sit straight up with two inches clear above me. It has been a big plus for me," he explained.

Jefferson, who spent more time ducking under doorways than bouncers, was forced to retire due to a rare hip condition in the summer of 2012.

Part Ten
– Change of scenery

42. Bat and ball

CURRENT Essex cricket coach Paul Grayson and his brother Simon were equally talented cricketers and footballers in their youth.

Although Paul became a first-class cricketer and Simon a professional footballer, both excelled at each other's chosen sport as teenagers.

Paul actually turned down the chance of a possible professional football career to pursue the opportunity of playing first-class cricket.

He played for Yorkshire before joining Essex and made two one-day appearances for England, before becoming first-team coach at his adopted county.

Simon played for Leeds United, Aston Villa and Blackburn, as well as loan spells at Sheffield Wednesday, Stockport County, Notts County, Bradford City and Blackpool.

He then managed Blackpool, Leeds United, where he was at the time I interviewed brother Paul about their sporting relationship in the summer of 2010, and then Huddersfield Town and Preston North End.

The Graysons were brought up in Bedale, a small market town near Northallerton about 45 minutes from both Leeds and Middlesbrough.

Paul recalled: "Simon played for Yorkshire School at cricket – he was a decent all-rounder, a fast bowler who would give it a bit of a slog down the order!

"And I played football to a decent standard as well and went to Middlesbrough, Newcastle, Sunderland and Leeds for schoolboy trials.

"I got offered terms by Middlesbrough at 16, but cricket was always my first love so I joined Yorkshire, while Simon joined Leeds United as an apprentice, as they were called in those days, at 16."

The Graysons are unique sporting brothers in that they both went into managing/coaching in their respective sports at the top level when their playing careers were over. Whereas Paul always had one eye on a possible future career as a coach, he said he was surprised that Simon had aspirations to be a football boss.

Paul said: "I thought he would make a good assistant manager or first-team coach, but I never thought he had that nasty streak in him to be a manager – he always seemed too nice for that!"

He said there was no sibling rivalry between the brothers, just a bit of friendly banter.

"Simon has had two promotions – one with Blackpool and one with Leeds – and we have had one promotion and won the Friends Provident Trophy, so we are two-all so far as the trophy cabinets are concerned at the moment!" he added.

Former Ipswich Town and Colchester United footballer Gavin Johnson is one of a host of ex-players who were also useful cricketers.

Johnson had been playing for local village side Stowupland for more than 20 years, but in the summer of 2010 he hit a rich vein of form that brought him three consecutive centuries in the MSC Suffolk Alliance.

After finishing bottom of the Suffolk Premier League the previous season, Stowupland had moved to the MSC Suffolk Alliance – and Johnson was certainly enjoying himself.

He scored 134 against Kesgrave Second XI, followed by 117 not out versus Coddenham, before recording a career-best 153 against Saxmundham Second XI in Section D.

Johnson, who was 39 at the time, batted at No.3 and described himself as 'an attacking batsman who likes to warm the fielders' fingers' once he got his eye in.

He told me: "It took me 19 years to get two centuries, before I scored three last season and have now scored three more this year, making it six in two years!

"The ball has been flying out of the middle this season. I have not been doing anything different, although obviously the standard is not as good as it was in the Suffolk Premier League."

Johnson's run of centuries had come to an end the weekend before we spoke, when he made a mere 78 against Stradbroke Second XI!

Mark Bailey was another sportsman who was talented with bat and ball, although in his case it was as a rugby player.

Bailey was a good club cricketer, indeed good enough to skipper Suffolk's Minor Counties side and claim 105 victims after making his debut in 1980, but he was an even better rugby player.

Not only did he play at full-back and on the wing for Wasps but also for England, although his international career certainly had its ups and downs.

I grew up with Bailey, attending the same primary school in Ipswich, and counted him among my closest friends, so he was always willing to co-operate over stories where possible.

Bailey made his international debut on England's controversial tour of South Africa in 1984, appearing in both Test defeats in front of crowds of around 70,000.

Stories surfaced about the England players drinking heavily on tour, something which Bailey strongly refuted when I spoke to him upon his return.

"Without a doubt, things have been exaggerated," he said.

"But there are always high spirits on a tour. You know what it is like when a bunch of lads get together. I am certainly not ashamed of anything that happened to myself or any other players."

Bailey was 'blacklisted' later that year for his troubles along with the rest of the squad for touring South Africa, but said he had no regrets.

A stress injury of the foot, aggravated by playing on the hard grounds when winning his first two caps, brought his blossoming international career to a halt.

He subsequently played against the USA in the inaugural 1987 World Cup in Australia, but his international career appeared to be over a year later.

Bailey launched a broadside at the Rugby Football Union, after missing out on joining England's summer tour to Australia for the second time in a fortnight!

He answered an SOS call on the eve of the tour in May to replace the injured Mike Harrison only to fail a fitness test on a nagging groin injury.

After regaining fitness he received a phone call asking him if he was available to fly out to join up with the squad as a replacement for the injured John Buckton, only to then be told to stop packing his bags.

The selectors had instead decided to call up Tim Buttimore who was already in Australia playing for Sydney side Manly.

Bailey let rip at what he called the 'most crassly inefficient, archaic, insensitive administrative process in this country' and with it appeared to kiss goodbye to ever being picked to play for England again.

The former Ipswich School pupil told me: "I will never again make myself available for an overseas tour for any England side. I am more dazed than hurt by what has happened.

"Disappointment comes from unfulfilled expectations – my expectations of sensitivity from the whole England set up were never high."

Don't forget, that back in 1988 rugby union was still an amateur game, and Bailey was working full time as well as in the middle of negotiations to buy a house.

But just five months after his outburst Bailey was named as skipper of the England B side to face Australia at Twickenham.

The 27-year-old Cambridge don said at the time: "I don't regard this as a return to favour or a springboard to a twilight return to international rugby."

But that is exactly how it panned out, Bailey being named as a replacement during the following year's Five Nations Championship without getting on.

He subsequently scored his first try in England colours in a 58-point trouncing of Fiji in November 1989, with Rory Underwood helping himself to five tries on the other wing.

Finally, in January 1990 – nine years after he was first named in an England Five Nations squad – he pulled on the jersey in the tournament.

That came in the 23–0 victory over Ireland, before he won the last of his seven England caps in the 13–7 loss to Scotland at Murrayfield just two months later.

43. *Wish you were here*

IT WAS mid-morning on a Monday in July 2004 when the phone rang on the sports desk at the Ipswich offices of Archant Ltd.

It was the *Mail on Sunday* calling.

Nothing unusual in a national newspaper calling a provincial sports desk, except this was different.

It was not a sports reporter from the *MoS*, but a member of the newspaper's promotions team.

My heart started to beat faster as colleague Dave Vincent put the caller through to my extension, as I had a pretty good idea what the call was about.

The previous morning I had spotted a competition in the *MoS* to win a holiday to Jamaica, with three runners-up prizes of a pair of tickets to the forthcoming Lord's Test between England and the West Indies.

The competition was run in conjunction with Sandals holiday resorts to mark the imminent Test Series between the two countries.

The caller informed me that not only had I won one of the three pairs of Test tickets that were on offer, but that I had scooped the main prize!

To win such a prize normally involves entrants having to answer a series of questions, but that was not the case in this instance.

To stand a chance of winning you simply had to phone the number in the *MoS* and leave your name and a daytime number you could be contacted on the following day.

It was one of those surreal moments when I was told that I had won – after all, we have all entered national competitions, but do you actually know someone who has *won* one?

My wife Juliet at first refused to believe me when I told her – and it was only when the confirmation arrived in the post a few days later that it finally sank in.

We chose to go to Sandals Royal Caribbean, one of three resorts situated in the Jamaican capital of Kingston, for our all-inclusive week-long holiday.

As if that wasn't enough, I was fortunate to be picked out of the hat for two plum Press trips during my time working for Archant.

Press trips would regularly be offered to the newspaper, with the recipient – sometimes just the journalist, other times accompanied by a partner – being wined and dined in return for writing an article to promote what was on offer.

Most were at locations in England, but some would be abroad, mainly in Europe, while occasionally something more exotic would be up for grabs.

The usual protocol was that the travel editor would make everyone aware and those that wished to be considered would go into a draw.

When a ten-day trip to the Eastern Cape in South Africa came up in September 1997, Juliet encouraged me to put my name forward.

The trip was for a journalist only, who would be among a party of ten travelling to four different locations.

Surprisingly, I was one of only nine Archant journalists whose names went into the hat – and even more surprisingly, my name was the one to be pulled out.

The odds of being selected were even greater – one in 15 – when a week-long trip to The Maldives was on offer in 2008.

You've guessed it, I defied the odds to be the lucky person to be chosen to represent Archant on the trip, where I was joined by three other provincial journalists.

Although it sounds like I must have been jetting off abroad to luxurious locations at regular intervals, I only went on seven Press trips – three in this country and four abroad – spread across nearly 32 years. That is put into perspective when you consider one colleague, sports sub-editor Daren Francis, went on three trips in a matter of just a few months!

However, trips to South Africa and The Maldives were two of the best trips that were offered during my entire time at the newspaper.

The Maldives remains the most idyllic place I have visited – a real 'wish you were here' location.

Although I experienced a few holidays abroad during my younger years it was not until the age of 25 that I got the travel bug – and that came about courtesy of my mate Tim Snook.

He had travelled to Australia in 1985 as part of the Great Britain cycle speedway team to compete against the hosts, and two years later was planning a return trip and invited me to go with him.

That month spent Down Under in early 1987 really opened my eyes and 18 months later I was off to the West Indies with Fred Rumsey Travel to take part in the annual Pro-Am Cricket Festival held on the island of Barbados.

There I played in a team skippered by David Holford, cousin of the great Garry Sobers, who was a useful all-rounder himself and played in 24 Tests.

Also in our team were Gloucestershire slow left-armer David Graveney – later to play for Somerset and Durham before becoming England's chairman of selectors – former Kent and England all-rounder Richard Ellison and Jon Ayling, who had broken into the Hampshire side as an all-rounder that year and went on to play six seasons for the county.

In our opening match against Chris Cowdrey's XI I was dismissed for just three by a player who was starting to make a real impact in the England Test team.

However, it was for his swashbuckling batting, rather than his leg spin, that Robin Smith is fondly remembered as an international cricketer. I also batted at Kensington Oval, the Test match ground in Barbados, when I went in on a hat-trick following the dismissals of Holford and Graveney and survived to enable my partner Ellison to reach his half century.

That match was against the team skippered by Yorkshire and England wicket-keeper David Bairstow, who was enjoying his honeymoon with his second wife.

Bairstow came across as the life and soul of the party, and it was with some surprise that I heard he had committed suicide ten years later.

My thirst suitably quenched I returned to Australia for a seven-week long holiday in early 1991, in which I saw more of the Lucky Country than some Australians do in a lifetime.

I had only been back in the country a few weeks when James Easter, whose company Travel Plus had organised my two trips Down Under, asked me to be tour manager for Ipswich School's Cricket Tour to Australia over the following Christmas and New Year!

So I joined the 18 boys and three masters who included former Essex spinner Ray East on the 23-day trip that started in Brisbane and ended in Sydney after stopping off at the seaside town of Port Macquarie.

By the time I returned it meant I had visited Australia three times in less than five years!

For my 50th birthday I wanted to do something special and so embarked on an 11-day trip with Juliet to Peru and Brazil, the highlight visiting Machu Picchu, which had been top of my list of 'must visit' destinations for a number of years.

In the autumn of 2012 when the post became vacant I put myself forward for the position of travel editor at Archant Suffolk, and was handed the part-time role in addition to my sports desk duties.

However, little did I know that when I booked myself and Juliet on a three-night trip to Jersey the following May, that it would signal the end of an era.

44. Signs of the Times

THE crowd that had gathered numbered several hundred as they jostled for position to keep abreast of events inside the Stadio Olimpico in the Italian capital of Rome.

They were eager to find out how their favourite team were faring against Lazio, in a second round, second leg tie in the UEFA Cup.

But, unlike today when football fans are able to follow the fortunes of their favourite teams in Europe via live coverage on Sky Sports, their laptops, iPads and mobile phones, this was a completely different scene.

No, the Ipswich Town supporters were standing outside the offices of the *EADT* and *Evening Star* in the town's Lower Brook Street. Looking at a blackboard. Waiting for updates to be chalked up.

If you hadn't travelled to Rome for the second leg of the tie in November 1973, it was the only way of getting updates from the match as they happened.

I was not among them – I was only 12 years old at the time – but the picture painted above came courtesy of Elvin King (a future colleague of mine for almost a quarter of a century) who was responsible for the updates.

Ipswich had been drawn against Real Madrid, one of the powerhouses on European football, in the previous round, and it was gone midnight and on BBC 2 before news was broadcast back in England that a goalless draw in the Bernabeu had sent Town through 1–0 on aggregate.

The *EADT* and *Star* decided to set up a phone service for the second leg of the Lazio tie, whereby the public could call one of a dozen phone ads lines during the match to hear updates.

But such was the interest that hundreds of supporters gathered outside the offices to see the scores as they were chalked up, blocking the street in the process.

Compare that scenario with the one just days before writing this chapter when I was sat in the stand at the Millfield watching Hadleigh United versus Felixstowe & Walton United in the Thurlow Nunn League Premier Division.

I glanced at the Twitter feed on my iPhone to see that there was a tweet posted at 3.08pm featuring a video clip of Ipswich Town striker Daryl Murphy's goal in the opening minute of that afternoon's Sky Bet Championship match at Brentford.

So just seven minutes after the goal was scored at Griffin Park it was available to view online whether you happened to be in Hadleigh or Honolulu!

It is a sign of the times how technology has altered the world we live in over the last four decades.

In the summer of 1981, when I started working for Eastern Counties Newspapers Ltd, as Archant Ltd was previously known, at the branch office in Felixstowe, we still used typewriters to file our copy.

Each day a van would arrive from head office in Ipswich in the late afternoon to drop off that day's late edition of the *Evening Star* and to collect the parcels containing stories and photographs for the following day's papers before returning to Lower Brook Street.

If you missed the van then you either had to drive back to Ipswich with the copy and/or photographs or put them on an Eastern Counties bus!

The bus stop was just up the road from our offices in Hamilton Road and the main Eastern Counties bus depot was a couple of hundred yards' walk from our head office in Ipswich.

This scenario was repeated at district offices all around Suffolk and occasionally someone would go to pick up a parcel and it would be nowhere to be seen.

Again, this was a far cry from the technology employed today, which allows reporters and photographers to email words and pictures via netbooks, laptops and iPhones within seconds.

That's always assuming you can get a signal to get an Internet connection!

All reporters and photographers will be able to recall tales of flying by the seat of their pants, thanks to eventually getting a connection just when they thought they never would.

Sometimes the technology does let you down – and we all know that as we have come to rely on it so heavily in our day-to-day work that when it does, the problem intensifies.

I encountered such a problem the night Ipswich Town played at Walsham-le-Willows in a Suffolk FA Premier Cup tie in November 2012.

Mick McCarthy had not long taken over as manager from Paul Jewell and he fielded an experienced side containing a number of first-team squad players against the Thurlow Nunn League Premier Division side.

A crowd of 745 turned up at Summer Road to see the likes of Michel Chopra, Jason Scotland, Nathan Ellington, Luke Hyam and Jay Emmanuel-Thomas in action in the first-round tie that Town won 5–1.

I had arrived at the ground early, not only to secure a car parking spot, but also to get my netbook (small laptop) set up and start writing my report by entering the team line-ups.

Walsham chairman Mike Powles showed me to where the club had run a cable off an extension lead into a portable building, situated behind the goal at the clubhouse end of the ground, which had a table and chair inside for me.

Everything was working as it should be before the match and I left my netbook there and took my seat in the stand in time for kick-off.

When I returned at half-time to start entering details of the first-half's play, my netbook had 'frozen' – and I was unable to get it working again either then or at the end of the match.

The only way I could file my report was to resort to the tried and trusted method of phoning it through to a copytaker.

Archant Ltd had dispensed with employing copytakers at night a couple of years before then, so it was fortunate for both the company and myself that I was able to call my wife at home at half-time and put her on standby.

Juliet was employed at the Ipswich offices as supervisor of the inputters (they did more than just take telephone copy) until she had taken voluntary redundancy in January of that year.

I was able to dictate my report over the phone (thankfully I was able to get a signal for my iPhone) for Juliet to type up using our computer at home, before emailing it through to the office.

It was only her goodwill that ensured Walsham's big night was fully recorded in the *EADT* and *Ipswich Star* the following day.

As I said, we take new technology for granted until it lets us down and then we have to think on our feet and find a way to solve the problem.

New technology has also had a major impact on the way we report news.

It is almost impossible to keep a story under wraps for even several hours for fear of it leaking out via social media these days.

When former Middlesex and England batsman Roland Butcher agreed to sign for Suffolk ahead of the 1991 season I was aware that he was due to do so before I went on holiday to Australia.

But as it was not a done deal as such, I agreed not to write the story until after I returned in case it fell through and Suffolk officials were left with egg on their faces.

On my first day back at work I duly rang Butcher and got some quotes from him for the story that appeared in the next day's papers nearly NINE WEEKS later!

There is no way, with the best will in the world, you would be able to sit on a story like that nowadays.

Social media is so instant and so many people have access to it that rumours and gossip spread like wildfire.

Someone once asked me what percentage of stories that I wrote came via seeing something on Twitter.

Initially I estimated it at around 40-50 per cent, but when I stopped and thought about it more, the answer was closer to 60-70 per cent!

More often than not it would be a non-league club releasing news of a new signing or managerial arrival or departure on Twitter, sometimes with a link to their website.

But occasionally it may be an announcement by an individual or even a cryptic message that could directly lead to a story.

How times have changed, but at least those Ipswich Town supporters who stood outside in the street waiting for updates to be chalked on a blackboard were rewarded.

Although they lost 4–2 on the night, Town's 4–0 first-leg victory saw the club progress to the third round of the UEFA Cup to herald the start of a golden European era for the club.

45. Sweet FA

LAURA Smith took up her post as the first female chief executive of Suffolk FA in December 2012.

The 33-year-old said it had always been her dream to work full-time in football when I interviewed her soon after at the county's headquarters in Stowmarket.

But it was not long before she was facing a storm of protest after Felixstowe & Walton United were thrown out of the Premier Cup, the most high-profile of the county cup competitions run by Suffolk FA.

A bumper crowd of 1,050 had gathered at the Goldstar Ground in early January to see the underdogs from the Thurlow Nunn League Premier Division deservedly defeat a young Ipswich Town side.

However, the Seasiders' joy at reaching the semi-finals following their 2–1 victory turned to fury after they were removed from the competition for fielding an ineligible player.

Felixstowe were found guilty of the alleged offence, after Tom Deller appeared as a substitute in the closing stages, and Ipswich Town were reinstated instead.

Deller had accrued five bookings and was therefore suspended for the tie, but because of confusion over the date of Deller's fifth caution, Felixstowe understood he was free to play.

Whatever the rights and wrongs, it was a headache the new chief executive could have done without. And it was about to get worse.

Ipswich Town were now due to meet Lowestoft Town in the last four of the competition, but the wet weather was playing havoc with scheduling the tie due to the backlog of fixtures and ground availability.

In an attempt to get the tie played, Ipswich Town agreed to travel to Lowestoft's Crown Meadow, rather than meet at a neutral venue, as it would generate extra revenue for the Trawlerboys. Both clubs announced the news on their respective websites.

It sounded like the ideal solution, except that Suffolk FA were going against their own competition rules, which stated the semi-finals should be played at neutral venues.

Both Bury Town and Leiston, who were due to contest the other semi-final, were up in arms and critical of the county's handling of organising the venues, which I duly reported.

In PR terms, Suffolk FA had scored a classic own goal – and coming on top of the Felixstowe & Walton United fiasco it only served to make matters worse.

It was soon after this that I received a phone call from Laura, who was, not surprisingly, keen to improve the county's standing in the eyes of the community.

While accepting that Suffolk FA could have handled both situations better, she said that these overshadowed all the good work the county did at grassroots level which did not get reported.

I said that if no-one made us aware of what was going on it would not get reported in the media.

Laura said she would like to meet my colleague Mike Bacon and myself over lunch to discuss the way forward. Bacon declined his invitation to attend the meeting, which was to subsequently change my life.

We met at The Lion in Needham Market and I reiterated that I felt the county needed to be more pro-active in providing information to the local media.

During the course of our conversation I mentioned that another round of redundancies had just been announced at Archant.

One member of the sports department would be made redundant under the proposed cuts, and I said that if the worst came to the worst,

I might be looking for another job in the near future. At that stage all I was interested in was trying to ensure that it would not be me receiving my P45 when the Archant axe fell.

So it came as a surprise to me to subsequently learn that Suffolk FA were looking to employ a marketing and public relations officer.

However, my focus was still on fighting to save my job – I was one of five sports journalists at risk – and did not really think much more of it.

It was only when I saw the job specification that the sands started shifting. When I looked through the job spec I warmed to the idea, even though it meant a cut in salary and the role was four days a week.

But by this stage I really fancied the idea of a fresh start and a new challenge, and at the age of nearly 52 I felt it was an opportunity too good to let pass me by.

I could have continued at Archant hoping I would not be the one to be made redundant and still ended up losing my job – and then what would I do if the position at Suffolk FA had been filled in the meantime?

Alternatively, I could have been kept on but then maybe found myself in a similar scenario 12 months later, when I would be a year older and it would be even harder for me to find alternative employment.

The more I thought about it, the more I thought I would regret it if I didn't take the plunge, plus the voluntary redundancy package on offer would soften the financial blow.

After nearly 32 years at Archant it just felt like the right time to move on. I had already been dubbed a 'lifer' at the newspaper – someone who spends their entire working career there – but I didn't fancy spending the next 15 years in the same job.

Plus I had always wanted to leave on my own terms – not be someone who was kicked out of the door because they had become a liability.

My decision was also a lifestyle choice. On the one hand my parents were not getting any younger and at the other end of the scale was Gabrielle, my recently-born first grandchild.

While I still enjoyed my job at Archant, most of what I really enjoyed was being done in my own time, so I was working longer and longer hours.

Working weekends and bank holidays had always been something I accepted as part and parcel of working in a sports department.

Now they were becoming a chore, and those nine-hour long shifts every second or third Sunday were a real slog and something I had started to begrudge when I would rather be spending some quality family time.

So I applied for voluntary redundancy on the proviso that I would take it if I got the job at Suffolk FA, which is just what happened.

On Wednesday, 15 May 2013 – the day after covering the Premier Cup Final – I finally left Archant, less than two months shy of 32 years' service.

The switch to Suffolk FA has suited me down to the ground. Within six months of making the switch I was offered full-time hours and as I write, two years on, I have never had any regrets over the move.

It has certainly been a case of Sweet FA.

Ends